Paperback ISBN 1904312225
ISBN 13 - 9781904312222
Published in the UK by MX Publishing
10, Kingfisher Close, Stansted Abbotts, Hertfordshire, SG12 8LQ

Performance Strategies For Musicians

How to overcome stage fright and performance anxiety and perform at your peak … using NLP and visualisation

A self-help handbook for <u>anyone</u> who performs ~ musicians, singers, actors, dancers, athletes and business managers and executives

David Buswell

About The Author

David Buswell runs *Virtuoso* Coaching, a consultancy specialising in helping musicians from all branches of the profession to achieve peak performance.

He has worked with high-achieving performers from the classical tradition at the Royal College of Music, London, with rock and pop musicians at Drumtech, London, and with indian classical dancers in Ontario, Canada. His private clients include classical, pop and rock instrumentalists, ensemble and orchestral players, singers, actors and dancers.

David was educated at Uppingham School, Leeds Polytechnic, Manchester University and the University of East London. He holds a postgraduate diploma in counselling and is qualified as a Practitioner and Master Practitioner in

Neuro Linguistic Programming [NLP] and as a NLP Coach. He is a member of the International Coaching Federation.

David is a pianist, church organist and choir trainer. He has been organist of several churches in Leeds, Assistant Director of the Bradford Choristers and has taken choirs to sing in a number of UK cathedrals.

Acknowledgements

First my thanks to Christopher Connolly of Sporting Bodymind for inviting me to work with him on the *Zoning-In* project at the Royal College of Music, London in 2001-2002 [1] and at an RCM summer school in Lugano in August 2002. And also to:

❏ Francis Seriau, Director and Founder of Guitar-X, Drumtech and Vocaltech, who asked me to deliver six modules on Performance Psychology to Master Performance students and so encouraged me to collect my very random thoughts, and refine and compress them into something passing for a structure.

❏ Aaron Williamon of the Royal College of Music and the *Zoning-In* project.

---

[1] This multi-disciplinary project gave rise to a book edited by Williamon, A., *Musical Excellence*, Oxford University Press, 2004 in which Christopher Connolly and Aaron Williamon write about the application of *Mental Skills Training* (pp 221 – 245) to the project

❏   Ian McDermott, Jan Elfine and their fellow trainers at ITS (International Training Seminars) who taught me all I know about NLP. I acknowledge their hand in this book and apologise (if it is necessary) for my shameless adaptation of NLP approaches, thinking and techniques.

❏   Angela McAdam-Thomson, and Tad James from whom I learned most of what I know about trance and hypnosis.

❏   The people who contributed to my musical education – Michael Holman, Jill Bean, Kenneth Baird, Keith Dennis, Dr Donald Hunt and Simon Carter.

❏   Those who set me on the search for my Self which has lead me to where I am now – in particular, Rona, but also The Findhorn Community, and the training staff at the Psychosynthesis & Education Trust, and my fellow students, Shirley Briggs, Georgie Howarth, Ruth Pimenta, and Jan Shepheard.

❑   Angela Le Strange Meakin who sat in my garden and urged me to pursue my vision.

❑   Riaz Rhemtulla, a quiet, calm presence throughout the conception and delivery of this book, for 'being there' (and for his magnificent cooking).

❑   Chris Bush, Helen Chapman and Rachel Alexander who encouraged me in the planning and writing of this book and Steve Emecz and Bob Gibson who had a significant hand in its production.

❑   And, of course, my students and clients who have consistently inspired and challenged me - and made me realise that this work is of value.

Further Assistance

As I say many times during this book, the techniques and exercises contained herein are but a starting point. As with any skill, they must be practiced so that they become second nature and are reinforced.

For many readers it will be sufficient to learn the technique, to practice it regularly and to use it in times of stress. For others, a DIY approach does not work as well as working one-to-one with another person, and, for you, there are two ways in which I can help you further:

1. You can attend one of my workshops during which you will have the opportunity to work with me personally;

2. You can arrange an initial consultation with me and follow-up sessions when I will guide you to acquire the skills you will need to carry you through your performing life with confidence.

Details of workshops and of the various ways in which you can contact me are to be found at my website www.virtuosocoaching.com

I look forward to working with you.

Performance Strategies For Musicians

1. MENTAL WELLBEING AND PEAK PERFORMANCE

Page

1 Musicians And Mental Wellbeing
- Being A Musician   2
- Mental Health   4
- How To Use This Book   8

2 Mental Skills Training
- What MST Is   10
- How MST Works   12

3 The Performing State
- The Ideal Performing State   24
- Theoretical Models Of The Performing State   25

2. DEVELOPING MENTAL RESILIENCE

4 Breathing
- Stress   39
- Why Breathing Matters   44
- How To Breathe   46

5 Relaxation
- What Relaxation Is   51
- When To Relax   53
- Relaxation Techniques - The Options   54
  - Autogenic Therapy
  - The Feldenkrais Method
  - The Alexander Technique
- DIY Relaxation   58
  - CDs And Tapes
  - Progressive Muscular Relaxation

o Shortened Progressive Muscular Relaxation
o Simple Relaxation Routine
o Cued Relaxation
o Self Hypnosis
❑ Guided Relaxation   68

6   **Visualisation And Mental Rehearsal**
❑ What Visualisation Is   75
❑ How Visualisation Works   77
❑ The History Of Visualisation And Mental Rehearsal   81
❑ Benefits Of Visualisation And Mental Rehearsal   82
❑ Developing Your Visualisation And Mental Rehearsal Skills   84
❑ Using Your Visualisation And Mental Rehearsal Skills   90
❑ When To Visualise Or Rehearse Mentally   94

7   **Changing State**
❑ Defining State   95
❑ Finding Your Baseline State   98
❑ Changing Your State   102
o Association And Dissociation
o Anchors
▪ Setting And Firing Anchors
▪ Chaining And Stacking Anchors
❑ Changing Negative Thoughts To Positive   116
❑ Changing Limiting Beliefs   118
❑ Silencing Your Inner Critic   126
❑ Transforming Fearful Experiences   132

3. PRACTICE AND PERFORMANCE

8   Practice
- The Art Of Practice   143
- Preparing And Organising   145
- Time Management   153

9   Pre-Performance
- Routines   157
- Mental Preparation   160
  - Circle Of Excellence
  - Piece Of Cake
  - Peak Performance Imprint
- The Week Before The Performance   173
- The Day Of The Performance   176
- At The Venue   178

10   Performance
- Concentration And Focus   181
- Managing Mistakes   191
  - Lapse Perception
  - The Language Of Lapses
  - Dealing With Mistakes
    - Before Performance
    - During Performance
    - After Performance
- Reviewing Mistakes   203
- Reframing Mistakes   208

4. POST- PERFORMANCE AND AFTER

11 Post-Performance

□ Post-Performance Review   211
    o   Post-Performance Feelings
    o   Winding Down
    o   Reviewing Successes And Setbacks

12 Over To You

□ It's Up To You Now   221
□ Building And Maintaining Mental Resilience   221

Performance Issues And Recommended Solutions

□ A List Of Exercises And Techniques   224

Bibliography And Resources   227

Index   229

1. MENTAL WELLBEING AND PEAK PERFORMANCE

Chapter 1
Musicians And Mental Wellbeing

Being A Musician

The life of a performing musician is a demanding one. A high level of technical skill must first be acquired and then maintained. Due to the constant and pressing requirement to earn a living, many musicians have busy lives based on a portfolio career consisting of performance, teaching, recording and freelancing. In between these demands must be squeezed the hours of practice necessary to maintain technical proficiency and to be fully prepared for the next engagement. Such a life is lonely: as well as the isolation of the practice room, there is also the travel to and from engagements, the nights away from home, and the reluctance to share performing difficulties with colleagues.

To be a performing musician is physically and mentally exacting. The musculature, respiratory system and vocal cords must be in top condition, and the long hours of playing and singing can lead to over-exertion and injury. On top of this is the requirement to be fresh and mentally alert. Talent (or technical competence), physical health and mental health are the three pillars on which performing success rests.[1]

---

1 Adapted from O'Connor, J., NLP & Sports, Thorsons, 2001, p. 9

PERFORMING SUCCESS

| TALENT | PHYSICAL | MENTAL |

This book focuses on the third of these pillars – mental health.

Mental Health

Mental health is a concept which is not much spoken of. In the 20th and 21st centuries, the focus of 'mental health experts' has been turned more toward mental illness than to mental health, but they are not different sides of the same coin.

It is possible to be mentally unhealthy without being mentally ill, to lack mental strength and resilience without necessarily suffering from a mental illness such as depression, schizophrenia or psychosis. Feelings of being overwhelmed or inadequate, of not being able to sing or play a particular piece or a specific programme, of believing that something is not possible are not symptoms of mental illness, but they are handicaps to performing excellence.

A mentally healthy person can be defined as one who functions effectively and successfully, is capable and competent, can handle normal levels of stress, engage in satisfying relationships, and lead an independent life; they will also demonstrate resilience and the ability to recover from adverse situations quickly.

While the mis-named "mental health" specialists attend to the causes and symptoms of mental illness, the field of mental health and its impact on performance has been given a significant amount of attention by sport psychologists. Sport psychology is a discipline which has been evolving since the 1950's. It aims to understand the psychological processes involved in the interaction of mind and body and to develop mentally resilient performers. As Sven Göran-Eriksson, the former England Football Manager, remarked:

"So little is required to be successful in sport. It's certainly mostly a matter of psychology and in the end it's that psychological difference that decides whether you win or lose."

Mental health is the difference that makes the difference. This psychological edge has been defined as:

"Having the natural or developed psychological edge that enables you to: 1) generally cope better than your opponents with the many demands (competition, training, lifestyle) that sport places on a performer; and, 2) specifically, be more consistent and better than your opponents in remaining determined,

focused, confident, and in control under pressure." [Jones, Hanton & Connaughton, 2002, p 209]

There is no more than a semi-quaver of a difference between music and sport, and a number of similarities:

"People "play" sports and they "play" music, yet both involve hard work and discipline. Both are forms of self expression which require a balance of spontaneity and structure, technique and inspiration. Both demand a degree of mastery over the human body, and yield immediately apparent results which can give timely feedback to the performer. Since both sports and music are commonly performed in front of an audience, they also provide an opportunity for sharing the enjoyment of excellence, as well as the experience of pressures, fears and the excitement of ego involvement." [Green & Gallwey, p vii]

You don't have to be sick to want to get better! You may already be an extremely proficient and capable performer and you may want to build on that expertise and become an even better performer, or a more consistent performer, or to enjoy your playing more; in which case this book is for you. It is a self-help guide to building and maintaining mental resilience using a variety of methods and techniques which collectively are described as Mental Skills Training. It will cover breathing, relaxation and visualisation as well as giving you the skills to enhance your practice, your pre-performance routines, your performance strategies and the ways in which you manage yourself after a performance.

How To Use This Book

This book is divided into three sections.

This section, the first, explains what Mental Skills Training is and discusses the performing state. Section two begins to develop your mental resilience; the format for each chapter is the same – a description of why the particular MST technique is important, when to do it and how to do it, including 'exercises' which are contained within a shaded area:

.... and are signified by a different typeface

Section three considers how you might practice more effectively and efficiently, before climbing through the foothills of pre-performance strategies, to the peak of the performance itself and scrambling down the other side to the plains of everyday living and working.

Chapter 2
Mental Skills Training

What Mental Skills Training Is

MST has evolved from sport psychology. The underlying belief is that the mind, body and emotions are inextricably linked, and that the mind is a powerful determinant of how the body performs. MST is about building mental toughness and resilience, and the good news is that it can be learned. Once learned, the consequent psychological consistency leads to performing stability.

The nine characteristics of the mentally resilient performer have been described by James Loehr [2] as being:

---

[2] James E Loehr. Mental toughness training for sports

1.   Highly motivated and self-directed toward success;

2.   Completely positive yet realistic about himself;

3.   In control of his emotions;

4.   Calm and relaxed, viewing pressure as a challenge, not a threat;

5.   Focused and concentrated;

6.   Self confident and incapable of being compromised;

7.   In control and fully responsible for his actions;

8.   Resolute and determined to succeed;

9.   Able to control and maintain the right level of energy.

MST involves the teaching of techniques which enhance performance. It is about developing strategies which minimise negative thinking and negative feelings. It is about (re)programming your mind and body so that you perform at a consistently high level. Achieving consistent performance is not about working harder, practicing for longer or exposing yourself to an increasing number of concerts, auditions or competitions; rather it is about developing the mental toughness which will enable you to be a more resilient performer.

The techniques of MST are not difficult to learn, but they do require practice in the same way as technical and musical skills. They are not a quick fix or a miracle cure (although significant change can be brought about in a short space of time). Once learned, the techniques can be used to develop and improve confidence and self belief; motivation; a positive mental attitude; focus and concentration; emotional control; relaxation; goal achievement; and stress management.

How Mental Skills Training Works

What you are thinking and what you are feeling affects your performance. Because mind (thoughts and feelings) and body are inextricably linked, this can become either a vicious or virtuous cycle:

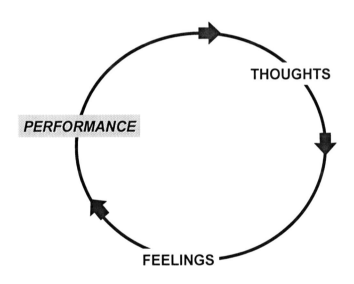

Thoughts and feelings are based on what you *imagine or interpret* from an event. Two players performing the César Franck A major Violin Sonata for their debut at the Wigmore Hall in London may imagine different things about the forthcoming performance, even though they are playing the same repertiore in the same hall in front of the same audience. The violinist might imagine that he is not capable of playing in front of such an august audience, in such a prestigious hall and on Radio 3; he may also believe that he is *never* sufficiently prepared. He feels nervous and uncertain. The pianist might regard the occasion very differently; he may think that this is the opportunity he has been waiting for all his life and he has every intention of enjoying every single minute of it. He feels confident and relaxed. These different thoughts and feelings will be reflected in their performance ~ the violinist's may be picked up by the audience as being shaky and insecure, whereas the pianist's may be heard as being secure but relaxed.

Violinist

THINKS:
Can't play well
Can't play here
FEELS:
Nervous
Uncertain
PERFORMANCE:
Shaky and insecure

AUDIENCE

Pianist

THINKS:
Lifetime opportunity
Enjoyable
FEELS:
Confident
Relaxed
PERFORMANCE:
Secure and relaxed

The same concert, venue and audience arouse two different responses with the consequence that there are two different performances. The bottom line is that if you, as a performer, can change the way in which you imagine your world to be, and you learn how to regulate your emotions, then you can achieve performing mastery. Henry Ford may have had performers like you in mind when he said

"Whether you think you can, or you think you can't, you're probably right."

What you are thinking and what you are feeling at this present moment is taking place in your conscious mind, but these thoughts and feelings are the result of a process of which you are not conscious. You think you will go and make a cup of tea (conscious), an action which may be prompted by any one of a number of unconscious motivations ~ thirst, a desire for comfort / warmth / nourishment, or an antidote to fatigue, etc. You feel nervous before a performance (conscious), a feeling which may be driven by sensations or memories buried in the unconscious ~ a fear of rejection, or of making a fool of yourself, or parental injunctions not to be a "show off".

The unconscious mind has a number of functions:

- It controls bodily processes (breathing, heartbeat, blood circulation, hunger, thirst);

- It is the source of dreams, creative ideas, intuition;

- It is locus of memory;

- It is the place where we retain our:
  - learned skills (e.g. how to turn on a tap),
  - instincts (e.g. self-preservation, sex),
  - motivation (e.g. falling in love),
  - emotions (e.g. joy, sadness, anger, compassion).

- … and it is a compelling driver of behaviour.

It is largely thanks to Freud that the unconscious has got a bad name for itself as the repository of base instincts and socially unacceptable desires. To be sure, these darker aspects may well be present in the unconscious, but it is more than that. It has light as well as shadow; it contains your potential, what you may become and it has the positive function of keeping you alive by regulating bodily processes. Although the unconscious mind may harbour murderous thoughts about parents, and unwanted sexual urges, it also ensures that you have sufficient oxygen, pump blood round your body as required, do not stick your hand in a fire and that you meet and mate, nourish and nurture. You cannot control these unconscious processes, but you can influence them to work in your favour. MST enables you to influence and change what happens in your unconscious and this changes your thoughts, your feelings and your behaviour … and improves your performance.

Hypnosis, which is part of the MST armoury, works on the unconscious mind by putting the subject into a trance and speaking directly to the unconscious mind (in crude terms, the conscious mind is bypassed allowing the unconscious to become more accessible). Hypnosis is commonly used to treat those who wish to stop smoking such that after one or more treatments the subject no longer craves nicotine; not only is the craving no longer there, they do not think about smoking, have a strong antipathy to the taste and smell of a cigarette and have positive thoughts about being a 'non-smoker'.

As with smoking, so with performing ~ the unconscious mind is where change takes place, the conscious mind where we become aware of the change and the consequent behaviour is how we know that change has happened. [3]

---

[3] From O'Connor, J., *NLP Workbook,* Thorsons, 2001

	Unconscious mind	Conscious mind	Behaviour
	Where change occurs	*Where become aware of change*	*How know change has happened*
Smoking	Messages suggested to the unconscious mind to stop smoking.	I don't want to smoke. I don't like the smell or taste of cigarettes.	Stops smoking.
Performance anxiety	Relaxing, confidence-building, positive thoughts suggested to the unconscious mind.	I don't feel anxious. I feel relaxed. I feel confident.	Confident, secure, relaxed and enjoyable performance.

The unconscious mind, although powerful, is mute. It does not and cannot speak. In the unlikely event of coming face to face with a tiger in your local high street, your unconscious does not communicate in elegantly constructed sentences. What it does do is give you immediate, clear and unequivocal messages through feelings. The unconscious mechanisms of the instincts, self-preservation and intuition gather up their skirts and initiate the acute stress response (also known as the fight or flight response) which triggers a whole gamut of bodily reactions which enable you either to stay and fight the tiger or run like heck; I prefer option two.

If the unconscious is powerful enough to stop the addicted smoker from smoking and can alert and equip the body for extreme danger, imagine how magical it would be if this power could be harnessed to improve your performance. To access this power requires only a light hypnotic trance. There are many myths surrounding hypnosis: for example, that it involves a pendulum, a man with a quiet soothing voice, and a subject on a couch; or, more sinister, that the subject has no control over their emotions and actions. None of these is true, since a light trance is no more than might be experienced when day-dreaming and it can be self-induced through breathing and relaxation. Once relaxed, the unconscious can be accessed through verbal suggestion or through visualisation.

And how magical too that the central nervous system does not distinguish between real and imagined events, and that it can be trained. Visualising a tiger in your high street can be every bit as terrifying as coming face to face with the beast; or imagining yourself playing a piece of music perfectly on your instrument is as effective a way of preparing mind and body for performance as playing it for real.

The three pillars of MST are breathing (Chapter 4), relaxation (Chapter 5) and visualisation and mental rehearsal (Chapter 6). Not only is each one of value in its own right, since the ability to breathe 'properly', to relax and to imagine are in themselves useful, but they are also effective weapons in the performer's arsenal, with the capacity to destroy fear and anxiety. Having acquired a knowledge of these techniques, you will learn how to change your thinking and feeling state (Chapter 7), how to put these and other approaches into use in your practice (Chapter 8) and in the three stages of a performance – pre-performance (Chapter 9), the performance itself (Chapter 10) and post-performance (Chapter 11).

Before moving on to these we will examine first the concept of the ideal performing state or the ideal set of thoughts, feelings and physical conditions that result in the optimum performance.

Chapter 3
The Performing State

The Ideal Performing State

NLP or Neuro-Linguistic Programming, which is a study of human excellence, pays particular attention to the "difference that makes the difference". Gregory Bateson, an anthropologist and one of the early gurus of NLP, believed that change and transformation come about through noticing the difference between one set of behaviours and another, and that this difference is information. If you want to discover what makes a good vocalist, one way to proceed (and possibly the most efficient) is to contrast the performance of a 'good' singer with a 'poor' one. The critical information is knowing what it is that the good vocalist does differently in his mind ~ the difference in his thinking and feeling states ~ and with his body; whereas discovering what they do that is similar is much less useful.

Theoretical Models Of The Performing State

There are at least two models of the ideal performing state. The first is from Joseph O'Connor, an author and a sage of NLP. He posits that three conditions are necessary to successful performance and he expresses these as an equation: [4]

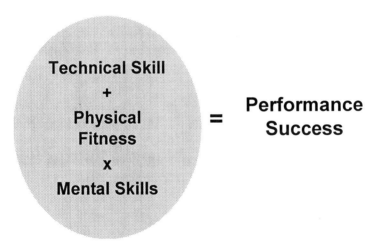

Technical Skill
+
Physical Fitness
x
Mental Skills

=

Performance Success

---

[4] O'Connor, J., *NLP & Sports,* Thorsons, 2001, p. 2

If you are a performing musician, it can be assumed that you have reached a high minimum level of technical skill. In order to play or sing, you will have achieved and, to some extent, will maintain a level of physical fitness. Both of these are the *sine qua non* of performance, but the difference that makes the difference is mental skills. The musician who develops and maintains mental toughness and resilience will not only transform his performance but will see improvements in his technical skill and physical fitness.

In O'Connor's model it is mental skills that are important (he shows it as a multiplier) and he identifies three aspects to mental skills:

1. Emotional balance: an equilibrium of relaxation and effort. Too much of one and too little of the other throws a performance out of balance. With an excess of relaxation, the playing is weak, there is a lack of power and it is difficult for the performer to concentrate. This is

most readily observed at its most extreme in the 'laid back' performer, where the player ambles on to the platform, undertakes some desultory tuning, and turns in a performance which is aimless, languid and inert. At the other extreme, the over-anxious performer bustles on to the platform, may well tune the instrument slightly sharp and delivers a performance which is tense, anxious and hesitant; too much effort is being expended and this creates tension, is wasteful of energy, and debilitating for the performer. The ideal performing state is one in which there is balance between relaxation and effort, where the performer is neither over- nor under-aroused, and in which both performer and audience experience the performance as relaxed but confident, natural and fluid, positive and enjoyable.

2. Will: this is not to be confused with the Victorian concept of the will, which is stern and forbidding and which condemns and represses other aspects of

human nature. The Italian psychiatrist and architect of the psychological theory of Psychosynthesis, Roberto Assagioli [5], described the function of the will as being ... :

> "... similar to that performed by the helmsman of a ship. He knows what the ship's course should be, and keeps her steadily on it, despite the drifts caused by wind and current. But the power he needs to turn the wheel is altogether different from that required to propel the ship through the water, whether it be generated by engines, the pressure of the winds on the sail or the efforts of rowers."

The will of the performer is indeed like the helmsman; it has a directive and regulatory function, balancing and constructively employing all the other activities and energies of the human being without repressing any of them. The key is that the energy is

---

[5] Assagioli, R., *The Act of Will,* Harper & Row, 1990, p 10

directed and regulated in such a manner that the outcome is the best possible performance.

3.   Concentration: is the "directing of the attention or of the mental faculties toward a single object" [6]. For the performer this is about being in the present moment, directing attention to what is important and dealing with distractions from within and without. The optimum performance will elude the performer if the focus is on past disasters, on present concerns or on future possibilities. 'What if I mess it up like I did in rehearsal?', 'I haven't got any food in the fridge', and 'Will I win the competition?' are less than helpful interference with the successful, fluid, enjoyable performance.

Interference is at the core of the second model of the ideal performing state. Tim Gallwey is the great high priest of the Inner Game; he created the concept of the Inner

---

[6] *Merriam-Webster's Medical Dictionary,* Merriam-Webster, Inc., 2002

Game Of Tennis, and extended this to encompass music, golf and other sports. The essence of Gallwey's theory is also expressed as an equation:

Performance = Potential minus Interference

As he writes in the Inner Game Of Music:

"The primary discovery of the Inner Game is that .... human beings significantly get in their own way; the point of the Inner Game is to reduce mental interferences that inhibit the full expression of human potential." [7]

Gallwey's thesis is that thinking interferes with optimal performance. This was most graphically illustrated in a challenge he accepted from a TV station in 1974. The test was to take a group of people who did not, could not and did not want to play tennis; among them was Molly Groger, a sedentary, overweight, 50 year old, magnificently attired in a moo-moo (for the uninitiated, this is a capacious, tent-like dress). Within 30 minutes she was playing

---

[7] Green, B., and Gallwey, W. T., *The Inner Game of Music,* Doubleday, 1986, p vii

forehands, backhands and serving with a panache and elegance that would shame tennis players of several months or years standing. Gallwey achieved this by throwing balls to Molly over the net and asking her to say 'bounce' when the ball hit her side of the court and 'hit' when she hit the ball with the racket. In this way, Molly was focusing on saying 'bounce – hit' rather than on her technique (or lack of it). Gallwey removed the interference by shifting Molly's focus from inside to outside, from thinking about forehands, backhands and serves to concentrating on the ball.

Both models demonstrate that what you are thinking affects your body and your performance. Sport psychologists claim that 50 to 95 per cent of success is due to mental factors and that the difference that makes the difference is 99 per cent psychological. As with sport, so with music: the difference that makes the difference is psychological. Mental fitness is as important in the arts as physical fitness and technical skill. For two musicians of equal calibre, it will be the difference in their mental skills that determines which will be the more successful.

Emmons and Thomas [8] list the main psychological characteristics of high achieving performers:

- o No feelings of fear;
- o An ability to regulate anxiety and arousal during performance;
- o Maintenance of positive thoughts and imagery throughout performance;
- o High confidence that is unshakable;
- o An ability to remain focused and concentrated, without distractions;
- o Determination to succeed;
- o Thinking that is committed and disciplined;
- o Control over the performance.

---

[8] Emmons, S., and Thomas, A., 1998. *Power Performance For Singers.* Oxford University Press, 1998

Where do **you** stand? What is **your** current performing state? Given below is a table which you should use to assess your current state with regard to technical, physical and mental skills. The three sections are further divided into 8 segments and you are asked to give yourself a 'score' between 10 (high) and 1 (low) for how satisfied you are with each aspect of your musical / performing life at this moment.

Ian, a violinist, scored his current levels of satisfaction as follows:

TECHNICAL		PHYSICAL		MENTAL	
Rhythmic accuracy	10	Stamina	6	Anxiety management	4
Technical security	8	Weight	9	Resilience	4
Dynamic control	9	Sleep	4	Relaxation	2
Intonation	8	Diet	8	Concentration	7
Articulation	10	Exercise	2	Enjoyment	7
Control of tone	8	Posture	8	Confidence	5
Bow control	9	Heart rate	7	Determination	7
Dexterity	8	Breathing	8	Positive thinking	3

This reveals that Ian is satisfied with his technical skills, scoring between 8 and 10; the scores are all high and there is balance with no wide variations between the individual scores. Ian's physical state has low scores for sleep and exercise, and Ian discloses that he does almost no physical exercise and has trouble sleeping because his mind is so active when he goes to bed – both of which have an impact on his stamina. The mental state profile shows Ian to be a determined performer, but he has difficulties with relaxation and positive thinking, with anxiety management, resilience and confidence.

In spite of his levels of anxiety, he gains enjoyment and satisfaction from his performance and, oddly perhaps, is confident. In discussion with him, he says that while he feels to be technically in control most of the time, he suffers from considerable anxiety just before and during the early part of a performance, when he finds it hard to recover from adversity. He makes a connection between his lack of exercise and sleeping difficulties and the problems he experiences in relaxing and managing his anxiety. He agrees to walk for 30 minutes a day on 5 days a week and we agree that we will work together on relaxation exercises to help him to sleep better and to give him resources he can use immediately before a performance.

So, what is your performing state?

It is important to be realistic in both the choice of

the factors on which you choose to rate yourself and in your scoring. If you are not a string player, then you will need to substitute another technical aspect for 'bow control'; if sleep is not a problem for you, but alcohol or smoking is, then include that instead.

I suggest that you fill this in quickly without deliberating on each score for longer than it takes to write it down.

TECHNICAL		PHYSICAL		MENTAL	
Rhythmic accuracy		Stamina		Anxiety management	
Technical security		Weight		Resilience	
Dynamic control		Sleep		Relaxation	
Intonation		Diet		Concentration	
Articulation		Exercise		Enjoyment	
Control of tone		Posture		Confidence	
Bow control		Heart rate		Determination	
Dexterity		Breathing		Positive thinking	

Now you know where you stand and what aspects of your technical, physical and mental state you need to work on. If you have technical issues, why not consult a colleague or seek help from a teacher? If you have physical issues, you may need to visit your GP or health practitioner who may well have a wellbeing programme for patients. If you have mental skills issues, then read on!

2. DEVELOPING MENTAL RESILIENCE

Chapter 4
Breathing

Stress

Optimum performance is inhibited by stress (or interference) and it has physiological implications – a fact which did not escape a character in a Woody Allen film who said, "I never get angry, I grow a tumour instead."

What is stress and where does it come from?

Robert Nideffer's stress model [9] states that the stress of a situation has physical and psychological implications which, in turn, have consequences for performance:

---

[9] From: Greene, Don., *Performance Success*, Routledge, 2002

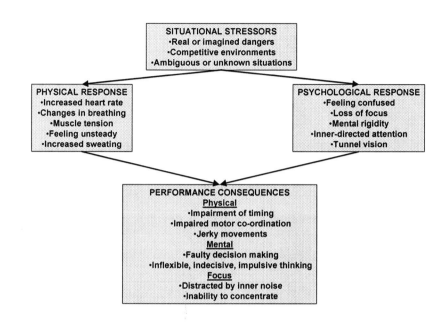

The physical and psychological responses are similar to those of the fight or flight model mentioned earlier. Also known as the Acute Stress Response, the fight or flight model was first described by Walter Cannon in the early 20th century [10].

---

[10] Cannon, W. B., (1914) The emergency function of the adrenal medulla in pain and the major emotions. *American Journal of Physiology* 33: 356-372 and Cannon, W. B., *The wisdom of the body*, 2nd Edition, Norton, 1939

To our cave-dwelling ancestors, the fight or flight response was an essential tool for survival, and it evolved over many thousands of years of living in wild and dangerous places. To us, living in the civilised world of the twenty-first century, it is often an ineffective response, which can actively prevent us from responding usefully to a problem situation. The noticeable and hidden effects of stress are illustrated in the following graphic [11]:

---

[11] Internet: Source unknown

Noticeable effects

•Pupils dilate
•Dry mouth
•Tense muscles
•Chest pain
•Palpitations
•Sweating
•Breathing fast and shallow
•Hyperventilation

Hidden effects

•Brain gets body ready for action
•Adrenaline released for fight or flight
•Blood pressure rises
•Liver releases glucose to provide energy for muscles
•Digestion slows or ceases
•Sphincters close, then relax
•Cortisol released (depressing the immune system)

Optimum performance is characterised by a balance between relaxation and effort. The Yerkes-Dodson law (so called because it was developed by Robert M. Yerkes and J. D. Dodson in 1908) [12] shows the relationship between the level of stress (or arousal) and performance. It proposes that performance improves with stress up to a certain point, after which levels of arousal begin to impact

---

[12] Source: http://en.wikipedia.org/wiki/Yerkes-Dodson_law

adversely on performance. It follows that there is an optimum level of arousal which will deliver maximum performance:

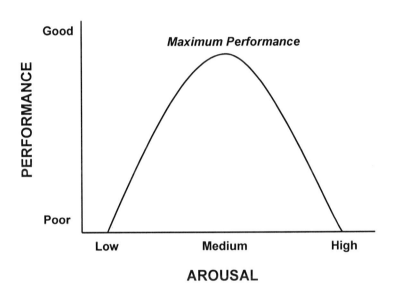

This optimum level of arousal, achieving a balance between too little and too much stress, can be achieved and maintained by breathing and relaxation (see Chapter 5).

Why Breathing Matters

Breathing is natural and we all do it. When breathing normally, the body is unconsciously restoring the balance between oxygen and carbon dioxide. Some people breathe quickly, and others slowly. Generally, quick breathers breathe less deeply than slow breathers. When under stress, breathing changes to being fast and shallow; this provides the muscles with oxygen to burn so that they are prepared either to fight or take flight. Fast and shallow breathing, or hyperventilation, creates an imbalance between oxygen and carbon dioxide:

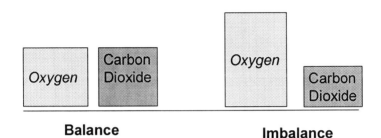

Balance

Imbalance

The imbalance created by hyperventilation can lead to:

- Tingling face, hands and limbs;

- Muscle tremors and cramps;

- Dizziness and visual problems;

- Difficulty getting enough breath;

- Exhaustion and fatigue;

- Chest and stomach pains;

- … and increased anxiety.

This is a vicious circle in which stress can lead to even greater angst; anxiety begets more anxiety.

How To Breathe

The solution is correct breathing, which:

- is gentle and even, smooth and flowing, not gulping or gasping;

- is through the nose, not the mouth;

- fills the lungs completely. Be sure to breathe into the abdomen / stomach area, not into the upper chest.

Correct breathing should be used all the time and not just when you feel to be under stress. Practice breathing! By practicing how to breathe properly it will become second nature. You should consciously breathe properly when anxious since:

Anxiety = Excitement minus Breathing

You can breathe consciously when you need to feel 'grounded' and, in an emergency, such as in the case of a panic attack, you can breathe into a paper bag to restore the oxygen / CO_2 balance.

Check your own breathing:

Lie on your back on the floor. If necessary, support your head and lower back. Make sure you are comfortable.

Place one hand on your upper chest (just below your pectoral muscles or breasts) and the other on your stomach (between your navel and your ribs). Breathe in and breathe out.

When you breathe in, does your hand rise or fall? Which hand rises and which one falls?

When you breathe in, your stomach should rise and when you breathe out, it should fall. If your chest is rising and falling, you are not breathing deeply enough, so take time to practice breathing into your stomach area. You can do this by holding your chest still with one hand and focus on drawing the breath deep into your stomach. If the chest continues to rise, place a weight (such as a heavy book) on your stomach and concentrate on getting it to rise and fall. If this fails and the chest is still rising while the stomach is stubbornly still, move on to all fours, like an animal. This will 'lock' the chest in place and compel the stomach to take over your breathing.

Important: Be careful not to force anything. If you feel dizzy or light-headed, return to your normal pattern of breathing and rest for a while before trying again in a few minutes. You are aiming to change a habit you have had for many years, so be gentle on yourself and your body.

Having checked whether or not you are breathing correctly, and having rectified any aberrations, you can move on to the next stage of breathing. The exercise below teaches you to breathe deep into your stomach or diaphragm and to make the out-breath longer than the in-breath. Lengthening the out-breath sends a message to the nervous system to relax; if you breathe in this way, your body has no choice but to relax.

Sit or lie comfortably on the floor with your head supported by a cushion or pillow.

Breathe in and out through your nose, fully (not shallow) and feel your stomach area swell as you breathe in and fall as you breathe out. Repeat the following 6 times, then take a pause and breathe normally, before undertaking another cycle of six:

- *First breathe out to empty your lungs*

- *Breathe IN to the count of 4*

- *HOLD your breath for the count of 2*

- *Breathe OUT for the count of 6*

- *PAUSE for the count of 2*

- *Repeat 6 times*

Breathing is the anteroom of relaxation. It is the process which begins the stilling of the body and the mind. It is why Yogis do yoga – the combination of the postures and the control of the breath are the precursor to meditation, which, like relaxation, is a form of trance.

Chapter 5
Relaxation

What Relaxation Is

Relaxation is the absence of activity and tension; a period of physical, mental and emotional stillness. As a word, relaxation has passed into common usage and its meaning has become distorted. For some, relaxation means 'chilling out', but this has a different meaning – it is time off work and the day-to-day grind of domestic chores; it means slobbing in front of the TV with a can of lager, drinking or going to the pub, playing sport, spending 'quality time' with partners or children. These things may be relaxing, but they are not <u>relaxation</u>, since they involve a degree of physical, mental and emotional stimulus. Even when supposedly 'switched off' the brain is actively engaged in the TV programme, the sport, or entertaining the children; while alcohol may be relaxing up to a point, it is also a stimulant.

True relaxation is achieved at the moment when the body, the mind and the emotions are still and not stimulated. In this state, two things happen, physiologically and psychologically: in your body, your heart rate slows down, your breathing becomes slow and regular, oxygen consumption decreases, the muscles relax and you feel calm in your body. The change in your body causes a change in your mind so that fear and anxiety drift away to be replaced by feelings of peace and wellbeing. It is impossible to be stressed and relaxed at the same time, since the body and mind are an interdependent system.

Relaxation can be learned, but to be learned effectively it must be practiced. Initially this should be done in low stress conditions, sitting or lying down in a quiet, warm and softly lit room, where you will not be disturbed. As your ability to relax increases, you can begin to practice in more stressful conditions until you reach the point where you are able to relax when highly stressed. This is the goal, to be able to still the body, mind and emotions when you are under significant stress, so that the balance between relaxation and effort can be restored to equilibrium.

When To Relax

You can relax when you want to:

•Fall into a deep and restful sleep;

•Experience and become aware of your own zero arousal level;

•Remain calm and conserve energy;

•Revitalise the mind and body;

•Rest and recover between performances;

•Recover from illness or injury;

•Experience a positive, pleasurable and beneficial state and to get more out of life.

This level of total withdrawal is not appropriate at all times and in all places (e.g. it is not advisable to withdraw completely as you walk on stage!) and relaxation also offers the option of withdrawing momentarily when you want to:

•Reduce over-arousal to a manageable level;

•Return to balance.

As a performer, you should relax momentarily when:

•Warming up before performance;

•When learning a new skill, technique or piece;

•When warming down after performance;

•Before imagery / visualisation.

Relaxation Techniques – The Options

There are a variety of ways in which to relax, and these are summarised below. There are relaxation methods which require another person to guide you through the process, but there are others which you can be taught to do yourself.

The three given immediately below can best be described as therapeutic relaxation, since they require the involvement of a trained teacher or guide. The information given is from their UK websites:

Autogenic Therapy

Autogenic Therapy was developed by the psychiatrist and neurologist Dr. Johannes Schultz (1884-1970).

AT teaches the individual a series of mental exercises which are designed to switch off the fight or flight response and to switch on the rest, relaxation and recreation system.

Following an initial individual assessment, the techniques are taught either one-to-one with a therapist or in a small group over 8-10 weekly sessions. Each session lasts about 90 minutes. You also practice the exercises for 10 minutes three times a day. For further information see: www.autogenic-therapy.org.uk

The Feldenkrais Method

The Feldenkrais Method®, with its focus on physical movement, is attractive to musicians who want to improve or increase their range of movement, or reduce the pain associated with movement, or who want to use the method to improve their general well-being.

It is named after its originator, Moshe Feldenkrais (1904-1984), an engineer and physicist as well as a Judo teacher. Apart from relief from muscular pain and easier movement, the method offers the benefits of relaxation, improved breathing and enhanced vitality. For further information, see www.feldenkrais.co.uk

The Alexander Technique

The Alexander Technique was first developed in the 1890s by an Australian named Frederick Matthias Alexander. He was an actor of some promise, but his career was jeopardised by the fact that he would become hoarse during performances to the point where he could scarce produce any sound. He attributed this to muscular tension in his neck and developed the technique to overcome his own problem.

An AT teacher helps the client to become aware of poor posture and retrains the body to move in a relaxed way without stress or strain. As with the two therapies above, the focus is on movement, but it has been found to be effective in treating stress and anxiety, as well as muscle tension, neck, joint and back pain. It is particularly popular with musicians whose instruments require they adopt postures which create physical stress. The AT website states that "Performers can improve stamina, increase clarity of perception, free up spontaneity and manage stage fright. Improved self-awareness allows them to get rid of poor habits and develop a wider repertoire of skills, to deliver the performance they envision". For further information, see www.stat.org.uk

D I Y Relaxation [13]

CDs And Tapes

The first DIY relaxation strategy is a halfway house between being guided by another person and being completely self-reliant. Regularly using an audio CD (or tape), most of which are typically a variation on a guided progressive muscular relaxation, is extremely helpful. The key word in the last sentence is 'regularly', since, like

---

13 The relaxation techniques described in the remainder of this chapter have been modified from a number of sources: PMR was developed by Dr Edmund Jacobson (Jacobson, E., Progressive relaxation, University of Chicago Press, 1938) and is used, inter alia, in material available from the Oxford Cognitive Therapy Centre (see www.octc.co.uk). I have modified and adapted them based on my own learning and experience with hypnotherapists and NLP practitioners.

everything else, relaxation needs to be practiced to be truly effective.

Progressive Muscular Relaxation

The progressive muscular relaxation was developed by Dr Edmund Jacobson in the 1920s and is used by a wide range of therapists [14]:

---

[14] Adapted from material from the Oxford Cognitive Therapy Centre, although other versions can be found on the internet (e.g. see www.youmeworks.com/relaxmuscles.html amongst many others)

Lie down in a warm quiet place where you will not be disturbed.

Wear warm but loose clothing, cover yourself with a blanket if necessary.

Breathe slowly and regularly through your nose.

Tighten each muscle group without excess strain on the in-breath for 5 seconds, release on an out-breath, and allow 10 to 15 seconds to notice the difference.

NB: Be careful not to over-exert yourself, especially when tensing the muscles in your feet and your back, since excessive tightening can cause serious problems. Tighten purposefully but gently.

Work in the following order: hands - arms - face - neck and shoulders - chest and abdomen - legs and lower back.

Finally do a scan of your whole body, checking to see if any muscles are still tense; the most likely candidates are your forehead, the muscles round your eyes, your jaw and *your shoulders – but there may, of course, be others! Imagine a golden light flowing into these tense muscles as you breathe in and the tension flowing out of them as you breathe out.*

When you are sure that every muscle in your body is relaxed, allow yourself to enjoy the experience as fully as you can.

Repeat softly to yourself the word "Relax" every time you breathe out.

Shortened Progressive Muscular Relaxation

Once you are an experienced and well-practiced PMR relaxer you can graduate to the shortened version[15]:

---

[15] Adapted from material from the Oxford Cognitive Therapy Centre

Gradually begin to:

Miss out the muscle tightening stage;

Move from lying down to sitting;

Change from a quiet environment to ones which are

progressively less quiet until, for example, you are

able to do this on a busy commuter train!

Simple Relaxation Routine

With regular daily practice, you will be able to master the above routines within several weeks, at which point you can move on to a simpler routine which you can use pretty well anywhere at any time [16]:

---

[16] Source: The Oxford Cognitive Therapy Centre

> *Imagine a soothing, restful image – a sound or word, object, place, or scene.*
>
> *Sit with your eyes closed.*
>
> *Imagine your body getting heavier and your muscles relaxing.*
>
> *Breathe in and out through your nose.*
>
> *On the out-breath, think about your image.*
>
> *Practice for 10 to 15 minutes.*

Cued Relaxation [17]

Remember Pavlov and his dogs? Pavlov began ringing a bell before placing food on the dog's tongue. Each and every time that the bell was rung, food was given to the dog. In time, the bell alone was enough to make the dogs salivate. This proved that all animals could be

---

[17] Source: The Oxford Cognitive Therapy Centre

conditioned to expect a consequence as the result of their previous experience. In psychology this is called 'classical conditioning'. It also has application to relaxation, although the bells and salivating are optional!

> *Choose a cue (e.g. a small coloured spot on your watch)*
>
> *Whenever you see the cue:*
>
> > *Drop your shoulders;*
> >
> > *Scan your body for tense muscles and let go;*
> >
> > *Check your breathing is slow and regular;*
> >
> > *Say "Relax" to yourself.*

Self-Hypnosis

Self-hypnosis is a process by which you can put yourself into a light trance state in which your muscles will relax, your pulse and breathing will slow down and your body will feel lazy and relaxed. It is NOT dangerous.

Because it is a self-induced trance, you are 100% in control.

Hypnosis, literally, means 'sleep'. When someone is in a trance they may appear to others as if they are asleep. Hypnosis cannot control anyone, nor can it make someone do something which violates their beliefs and values. The TV or stage hypnotist, who appears to exercise total control over his subjects, has carefully selected from the audience only those people who want to come onto the stage and provide entertainment to (or humiliate themselves in front of) others.

Two approaches to self-hypnosis are described below. The first is from NLP: [18]

Sit or lie down, uncross legs, arms, feet.

Breathe fully through your nose.

Begin by describing:

---

[18] O'Connor, J., *NLP Workbook,* Thorsons, 2001

3 things you can see

3 things you can hear

3 things you can feel

Then describe:

2 things you can see

2 things you can hear

2 things you can feel

Then describe:

1 thing you can see

1 thing you can hear

1 thing you can feel

Now close your eyes and concentrate on making your visual field as black as possible.

Feel the part of your body that is most comfortable.

Imagine that feeling spreading like warmth through the whole of your body and relax.

Let your mind wander gently, allowing your thoughts to pass by like clouds in the sky.

Bring yourself gently back into the room.

The second method of self-hypnosis is called the 4 step approach:

Step	Stage	Process
1	Fixation	Focus your attention on an object. The most commonly chosen objects are a candle or a black spot on a piece of paper.
2	Relaxation	Use a relaxation technique e.g. the shortened PMR given above.
3	Receptivity	Notice what you are feeling and thinking. Are you feeling relaxed? Is your mind quiet?
4	Repetitive suggestion	Choose a _positively expressed_ suggestion you want to implant

		in your unconscious mind.
		Invite your unconscious mind to
		listen: E.g. "I am a skilled
		player. I always play my very
		best" .... Repeat .... Repeat...
		Repeat.

Guided Relaxation

This is a guided relaxation which you might want to record using your own voice. If you do opt to do this, I recommend that you record it in a soft, silky voice and that you do not bark military-style commands into your recorder. Do not, of course, listen to the tape while driving your car or when operating heavy machinery (like a double bass).

Find somewhere to lie down where you will be warm, comfortable and undisturbed. If necessary put something under your head to support you and cover yourself with a

blanket to keep yourself warm. Lie with your feet about 6

inches apart and with your arms by your side with your

palms facing upwards. Let any sounds inside or outside the

room just float by like clouds in the sky.

First breathe out to empty your lungs.

Breathe IN 2, 3, 4; HOLD, 2; , breathe OUT 2, 3, 4, 5, 6;

PAUSE, 2.

IN 2, 3, 4; HOLD, 2; OUT 2, 3, 4, 5, 6; PAUSE, 2.

IN 2, 3, 4; HOLD, 2; OUT 2, 3, 4, 5, 6; PAUSE, 2.

Now breathe normally, noticing your stomach rise as you

breathe in and fall as you breathe out. Allow your body to

sink into the floor and feel yourself becoming heavy.

Now imagine a warm golden light flowing down into and

over the top of your head, into and over your forehead,

your eyes, relaxing all the muscles round your eyes, flowing into and over your ears, your nose, your cheeks, your mouth. Keeping your mouth closed, allow your jaw to sag; feel the tension around your jaw flowing away. Feel the warm golden light flowing down the back of your skull and into your neck and your shoulders. Relaxing and letting yourself go. Relaxing and letting yourself go. That's right.

And now the warm golden light is flowing down into your upper arms, your elbows, your lower arms, your wrists, your hands and down to the very tips of your fingers. Your head and your arms are feeling very relaxed. As your body relaxes, your mind relaxes. Relaxing and letting yourself go, relaxing and letting yourself go. That's right.

The warm golden light is flowing into and over your chest, down into the area round your heart, relaxing your heart muscles, into your stomach, relaxing your digestive system, down into your hips. The warm golden light is flowing down your back, relaxing all the small and large muscles in your back, down into your buttocks and your pelvis. Relaxing and letting yourself go. Relaxing and letting yourself go. That's right. Now the whole of the upper half of your body is feeling heavier, becoming limp and relaxed. Relax. Relax.

Now the warm golden light is flowing down into your thighs, relaxing all the muscles in your thighs, and down into your knees. All your muscles are relaxing. Your body is becoming heavier and sinking deeper and deeper into the floor. As your body relaxes, your mind relaxes. Any thoughts you have, let them pass like clouds.

The warm golden light is flowing into and over your

calves, your ankles, your feet and down to the very tips of your toes.

The warm golden light is flowing into and over your body, from the top of your head, down into your fingers and right down to the tips of your toes. You are very relaxed. Your body is sinking deeper and deeper into the floor. You are limp and relaxed like a rag doll. As your body relaxes, your mind relaxes. You are feeling very calm and very still. Notice any areas of tension in your body, and allow the tension to just flow away through your fingers or toes, down into the floor, deep down into the earth. Relaxing and letting yourself go, relaxing and letting yourself go.

I am going to count from 10 down to 1 and for every number I count, the relaxation in your body will triple. 10, relaxation tripling, 9, 8, 7, relaxation tripling, 6, 5, 4, relaxation tripling, 3, 2, 1. The relaxation in your body has tripled many times over. You are feeling very, very calm and very, very relaxed. That's right.

Enjoy this feeling of calm. Enjoy this sense of deep, deep relaxation.

Breathe slowly and gently. Every time you breathe out, your body becomes more and more relaxed.

[Relax for as long as you feel comfortable]

I am now going to count from 1 to 10 and when I get to 10 you will open your eyes and come back into the room, refreshed, relaxed and alert.

1 – 2 – 3 // 4 – 5 – 6 // 7 – 8 – 9. Coming back into the room, eyes open. 10.

You can anchor this state of relaxation (see Chapter 7), just before you hear the count from 1 to 10 bringing you back to conscious awareness. You can do this by, for example, using a physical anchor such as gently squeezing the ring finger on your left hand with the thumb and forefinger of your right; or auditorily, by saying quietly to yourself "Relax". Whenever you need to be more relaxed, fire this trigger by squeezing the finger in the same way, or by saying "Relax".

Chapter 6
Visualisation

What Visualisation Is

Visualisation is a sturdy weapon in the armoury of the mentally robust. It has the power to transform: to change failure into success, hopelessness into hope, and despair into delight. It can be used to overcome fear, to achieve goals, to build self-confidence and self-esteem. For the musician, visualisation is a compelling complement to physical rehearsal and practice, and, sometimes, a substitute for it. As with many of the skills taught in this book, it requires practice, but once the skill is embedded, it is there as an ally for a lifetime.

Many of us think visually. If you think back to your last holiday, how do your remember it? In words? Sounds? As a sensation in your body? Or in pictures? My most recent holiday was in New York in the heat and humidity of an east coast August; when I think of it now, it is in a series of images ~ the subway, standing at the top of the Empire State, walking round the site of the World Trade Centre, arguing with my partner on the Staten Island ferry, etc. This brings the holiday back to me in a very intense way. Not only can I see it, but I can feel the heat and smell the emanations of the subway; I can see, taste and smell the cocktails we had before we ate our 16oz steak and chips.

The step from thinking visually to visualisation is a small one. It formalises something which you have been doing most of your life; it provides a structure within which the power of visual thinking can be harnessed, and a framework within which the visual material can be customised, adapted and modified to produce a desired outcome.

For the performing musician, the most important aspect of visualisation is its use as a Mental Rehearsal

[MR] technique. This chapter is devoted to Mental Rehearsal.

MR is the mental or imaginary rehearsal of a physical skill without physical movement, using visual (seeing), aural (hearing) and kinaesthetic (feeling / touch) senses to create or recreate an experience similar to a physical event. The process is very simple: you begin by watching yourself on a movie screen in your imagination onto which you consciously summon, and then guide, daydreams in which you appear; these guided daydreams usually have a specific outcome (E.g. learning new repertoire or preparing for a performance).

How Visualisation Works

Although a very sophisticated mechanism, the central nervous system does not differentiate between real and imagined events. Have you ever woken from a nightmare in a sweat with your heart pounding believing that the strangler who is approaching your bed is now actually in your room? Or that you are about to step onto the stage to play a piece you have never heard or seen before on an instrument you have never played? You have been having a dream, but your nervous system has been behaving <u>as if it is real</u>. My experience is that these really vivid nightmares or dreams can take a while to recover from. This is because they have impressed themselves upon your visual memory and your muscle memory; the mental images have primed the body for physical action.

Mental rehearsal is another type of dream (and most certainly should not be a nightmare) which creates connections between the mind and the body that produce smoother and more precise physical movement in actual performance.

Research in the field of sport psychology shows that muscular movement during MR is equivalent to movement during actual performance. The significance of this is that a musician can mentally rehearse a piece and impress it in the muscle memory in the same way as it would be imprinted if it was actually being played; at the same time it is also being imprinted in the auditory memory. If you visualise yourself playing a piece, you may see, hear and feel yourself in the same way as if you were actually playing it. Dr Edmund Jacobson, who developed the Progressive Muscle Relaxation technique described in Chapter 5, also discovered that if the subject imagined tensing and relaxing the muscle groups, those muscles could be relaxed without any tensing or relaxing taking place; just to imagine them relaxing was good enough.

Visualisation speeds up the learning process. The purpose of practice is to prepare and programme the brain to send messages to your muscles so that a physical movement can be executed as proficiently and smoothly as possible. Mental rehearsal allows you to make these same connections in a way that would not be possible if you were to think about (rather than imagine) playing the piece; analysis impedes rather than facilitates the learning process.

The power of the imagination is well expressed by the golfer Jack Nicklaus [19]:

"I never hit a shot, not even in practice, without having a very sharp, in-focus picture of it in my head. It's like a colour movie. First I "see" the ball where I want it to finish, nice and white, sitting high up on the bright green grass. Then the scene quickly changes, and I "see" the ball going there: its path, trajectory, and shape, even its behaviour on landing. Then there's a sort of fade-out, and the next scene shows me making the kind of swing that will turn the previous images into reality ... I believe a few moments of movie-making might work some small miracles in your game".

---

[19] Jack Nicklaus, *Golf My Way,* quoted in Baum. K., *The Mental Edge,* Perigee, 1999, p44

The History Of Visualisation And Mental Rehearsal

Visualisation and mental rehearsal have emerged from the concept of 'guided imagery' developed in the 1930s and 40s by Hans Happich. Guided imagery is used in systematic (i.e. not free) meditation and in psychotherapy to access the contents of the unconscious mind. One of the more startling uses of visualisation was in the treatment of cancer by Carl and Stephanie Simonton in the 1980s. They found that cancer patients who used visualisation had a better prognosis than those who did nothing. These observations had been made by the Simontons at their Cancer Counselling and Research Centre in Dallas, Texas, and recounted in full in their best-selling book [20].

---

[20] Simonton, O. C., Simonton, S. M., and Creighton, J. I., *Getting Well Again,* Bantam, 1992

Benefits Of Visualisation And Mental Rehearsal

There are several reasons why musicians should employ mental rehearsal techniques.

The first of these is to improve physical functioning; as mentioned above, MR sends messages through the nervous system to muscle groups, preparing and programming the brain, laying down the connections to muscles and hardwiring the system for future action. MR tells the brain as accurately as possible how to organise the movement of the body.

MR helps you to change your emotional state - to calm your nerves, to get more energy and confidence before performance, and to relax and wind down after a performance.

Visualisation accelerates learning, makes the acquisition of new skills easier and helps with solving problems.   It is a valuable supplement to, but not a substitute for, physical rehearsal, especially where there is a danger of over-exertion (such as straining of the voice or over-taxing muscle groups).

Mental rehearsal can be used as a substitute for practice when you are injured and unable to play physically. Further, it helps you to:

- commit repertoire to memory;
- make your practice more efficient;
- heighten your sensory awareness (for example, to become more aware of tone, expression, intonation etc.);
- become more interested and involved in the music;
- build your overall confidence and mental robustness on stage;

- project your feelings out to the audience so that you make a connection with the listener(s);
- perform at your peak by mentally rehearsing your 'greatest hits' or past peak performances.

Developing Your Visualisation And Mental Rehearsal Skills

Not everybody is visual. Rather than 'seeing' things, there are people who hear things, feel them in their body or sometimes, but rarely, taste or smell them. Visualisation is not difficult, but it does give some people difficulty. The good news being brought from Aix to Ghent is that it can be developed. Try the following:

- *Close your eyes. Sit with your feet on the floor with*

your hands resting loosely in your lap.

- *Breathe out and then IN to the count of 4, HOLD for the count of 2, breathe out to the count of 6, pause for the count of 2 and repeat the cycle 3 or 4 times. Make sure that you do not exaggerate your breathing and that the out-breath is longer and slower than the in-breath.*

- *Take a moment to relax, check the areas of tension in your body and allow the tension to float away.*

- *Imagine each of the following in turn:*

- *SEE: the sun rising from out of the sea; the face of your best friend.*

- *HEAR: a nail being hammered into a piece of wood; a dog barking in the distance.*

- *FEEL: your hands being warmed in front of a log fire; snow falling on your face.*

- *SMELL: freshly baked bread; leather.*

- *TASTE: the segment of an orange; a sip of coffee.*

Notice which of these you found easy and which more difficult. If you found it more difficult to see, do not be put off. Try again, allowing random images to come into your head and rather than aiming to 'see' an image, 'think' about it instead.

These visual skills can not only be developed but need also to be controlled (in the sense that they can be manipulated for maximum effect). The brighter, sharper, clearer the images you can generate, the more influential will be their impact on your unconscious mind.

- *Close your eyes.*

- *Begin with breathing and relaxation, using the now*

familiar pattern of IN 2, 3, 4; HOLD, 2; OUT 2, 3, 4, 5, 6;

PAUSE, 2.

•*Open your eyes and look at an object near to you.*

•*Gradually close your eyes and imagine the object in front*

of you.

•*See the colour as vividly as you can, make it brighter,*

sharper, clearer.

•*Make the object smaller, distant; then larger, closer.*

Zoom in and zoom out.

•*Imagine yourself floating up to the ceiling and look down*

on the object.

•*Imagine yourself on the floor looking up at it.*

•*Imagine turning the object upside down.*

•*See it from the back, the front, from the inside.*

•*Open your eyes.*

Now that you are able to control the perspective from which you can see images, move on from seeing the image externally (this is known as 'dissociated'), as if it is on a movie screen, to actually being in the image ('associated'). This is an ability worth acquiring as it enables you to control the intensity of the experience you are visualising: rather than seeing yourself giving a perfect performance as if you are in a movie, it is more powerful to mentally rehearse that perfect performance as if you are inside your own body, seeing what you see, hearing what you hear and feeling what you feel.

The following exercise will give you the experience of visualising from a dissociated and then an associated perspective.

* *Close your eyes.*

* *Begin with breathing and relaxation: IN 2, 3, 4; HOLD, 2;*

OUT 2, 3, 4, 5, 6; PAUSE, 2.

• *Imagine yourself sitting in a cinema.*

• *See yourself on the screen, playing your instrument (Dissociated).*

• *Slowly zoom in and make the image brighter, sharper, louder, clearer.*

• *Turn the image into black and white; and then back into colour.*

• *Slowly zoom out and make the image more distant, duller, softer, less focussed, quieter.*

• *Imagine floating out of your body and up into the image on the screen (Associated). Seeing what you see, hearing what you hear, feeling what you feel ~ from inside your body.*

• *Open your eyes.*

Using Your Visualisation And Mental Rehearsal Skills

You are now ready to put your visualisation skills to work in the context of musical performance and there are some basic rules to be aware of before you begin:

> *•Always, always begin with breathing and relaxation, using the now familiar pattern of IN 2, 3, 4; HOLD, 2; OUT 2, 3, 4, 5, 6; PAUSE, 2.*
>
> *•Rehearse specific skills or qualities (emotional, physical or sensory) which you are working on in your technical and musical training or to 'future pace' issues you anticipate coming up.*
>
> *•Be positive: move towards what you want, <u>not</u> away from what you don't (e.g. 'I want to play smoothly'; NOT 'I want to stop playing raggedly').*

Be specific: imagine as much detail as you can ~ the venue, your clothes, any sounds or smells, the skill you are rehearsing.

See, hear and feel perfection: don't be satisfied with second best ~ imagine everything exactly as you want it to be.

Use all of your senses: sound, sight, bodily sensations, emotions.

Ideally, visualise externally (dissociated) until you have the images which are 'right' and then visualise internally (associated).

Now is the moment! Choose what you want to rehearse mentally, be aware of the ground rules above, and follow the sequence below.

• *Close your eyes; breathe and relax.*

• *See yourself (dissociated) in an ideal place for you to practice, create as much detail as possible, add in any friends or colleagues you want to support you.*

• *See yourself (dissociated) approaching your instrument.*

• *Begin to play / sing using the technique or piece of music you want to practice. See yourself doing it perfectly (or use someone else as a model). Notice what you can see, hear and feel as you observe yourself. How do you use your arms, head? How is your body positioned? How do you use your legs and feet?*

• *When this image is perfect, take a deep breath and watch the scene from somewhere else – nearer / farther, front / sideways / behind etc.*

• *Only when this image is perfect in every detail and you*

> *are executing the technique or piece of music perfectly, step*
>
> *inside the image of yourself (associated).*
>
> *• Mentally rehearse the skill you are practicing. Enjoy the*
>
> *feeling ~ you are playing perfectly!!*
>
> *• If you are not fully satisfied with the image, go back and*
>
> *dissociate until you are satisfied and then associate again.*
>
> *• Repeat the associated image at least five times ~ this will*
>
> *become easier the more you do it.*

It wasn't so difficult, was it? Like any skill, it will become easier the more you use it and the more you practice it.

When To Visualise Or Rehearse Mentally

It is better to practice visualisation and mental rehearsal regularly, especially in the morning (when it is more effective), and to do short, regular sessions, rather than long irregular ones late at night. Needless to say, you should not attempt visualisation while, as it says on the medication, driving, using machinery (such as a Tuba) or under the influence of alcohol.

Chapter 7
Changing State

Defining 'State'

State is a word which is used frequently in NLP (Neuro Linguistic Programming). A state is a snapshot of your current mental and physical processes and is important because your state determines your behaviour.

What is my present state as I sit writing? If I awake to sunlight streaming through the curtains and the sounds of the dawn chorus, I will leap out of bed, make myself a small cup of coffee, take the dogs for a brisk walk, return home and set about my writing with enthusiasm and vigour; if, on the other hand, I wake sluggish and tired, drag myself to the bathroom, skip breakfast, have negative thoughts running through my mind, I will sit down at my desk with a heavy heart and struggle to begin (never mind complete) my work.

States also filter and affect experience: in my sluggish, bad tempered state, I will effectively filter out pleasurable experiences ~ an offer of some work may be interpreted as yet more drudgery; good news from a friend may be filtered through my negative perspective and I may well be thinking "Hmm, she gets all the luck". When I am in a positive and happy state, I will most likely filter out unpleasurable experiences – the offer of work will boost my self-esteem and I will anticipate the fulfilment of that work with excitement; my friend's good news will be received with delight and joy.

States are influential. What I am thinking and feeling will influence significantly my view of the world and my performance in it. It is not unusual to get stuck in states and the invitation to 'snap out of it' will meet with a tart riposte. States are not immutable, *they can be changed* even though we may feel they can't. Sometimes it seems as though states just appear – you wake up feeling grumpy or happy; you are gripped with fear and dread when you enter the concert hall; you are filled with joy as you meet a close friend.

States are a choice. You a l w a y s have a choice – you can stay in your present state or you can change it to a neutral state or a resourceful one. In this chapter, you will learn ways in which you can easily and quickly change your state from a negative and un-resourceful one to one which is positive and resourceful. This is a precious skill for the performing musician; to be able to change state at will, to flip from being tense, uncertain and uncomfortable to being calm, confident and assured, and to be able to do this whenever you want is to be prized as highly as your musical talent and the skill with which you have developed and nurtured it.

Finding Your Baseline State

So, to work! First, let's find out about your baseline (i.e. normal) states. You will need to do the exercise below twice: once for your baseline everyday state (e.g. when at home, out shopping, at work, in the car etc) and again for your baseline performing state.

Your baseline performing state is not the same as your current performing state (see Chapter 3); your baseline performing state is your normal, 'everyday' feelings when performing, whereas your current performing state is how you are feeling right now about a performance. For example, you have a performance today which, due to additional internal or external pressures, may cause your current state to be one of high anxiety, whereas your typical baseline state when performing may be calm and relaxed. Talking about your state brings it into your conscious awareness, so find a friend who is prepared to spend time asking you the following questions. Failing this, take the time to write down the answers to the questions ~ do not rush the process, but be willing to go back and review what you have written, adding in anything that occurs to you. [21]

> - *Typically, how do you feel? If you find this difficult to define, rate yourself on a scale from 1 (low) to 10 (high) on the following ~ physically alive, mentally alert, emotionally happy; having done this try and find a single word which encapsulates all the elements of this snapshot. For example, if you have scored 9 on all factors, you might describe your baseline state as 'fizzing' or 'ecstatic'; on the other hand, if you scored 2 across the board, you may define your baseline state as 'low' or 'sluggish'.*

---

[21] Adapted from The NLP Practitioner Programme course material, © Ian McDermott (2002-3)

- *Where does this baseline state come from, by which I invite you to be clear about whether it is your state, or someone else's? (Be careful not to blame your state on someone else. Yes, there will be occasions when your state is influenced by your partner's daily misery or happiness, but, ultimately, you are responsible for your own state).*

- *Or did you learn it? Consciously or unconsciously? Who from? States can be learned from, for example, parents, teachers or spouses. If you always feel 'fizzing' (or grumpy), try and identify if this is a state you learned.*

- *Physically, what do you feel like in your baseline state? Be as specific as you can. Where do you have the physical sensations associated with this state? How intense are they?*

- *Mentally, what are you thinking about in this state? Again, be specific.*

- *Emotionally, what are you feeling in this state? Be specific.*

- *Who are you in this state? Are you truly yourself, or are you someone else? Who?*

- *What are your beliefs about this state? "I believe this state is ….."*

- *What are your beliefs about changing this state? "I believe that changing this state will ….."*

- *What are your capabilities in this state? What can you do or not do?*

- *How do you behave when you are in this state?*

- *Where and when is it appropriate for you to be in this*

> *state? It is appropriate to have a baseline state of '*
>
> *scared' when doing your first parachute jump, but*
>
> *probably not appropriate to be constantly anxious if*
>
> *you are a professor in a conservatoire.*

- *Now repeat the exercise for your baseline performing*
  state

Changing Your State

There are some very obvious and simple ways to change state. If you have ever been sitting at home feeling dejected and a friend calls to invite you to go to their house / the cinema / the pub / out for a meal, you may have noticed how quickly your state can change. Some easy state-changers are:

> *•Tell a joke – laughter changes your breathing and this*

> *alone has an impact on your body.*
>
> • *Move, walk, run, jump up and down, stand up, sit down, go into another room.*
>
> • *Distract yourself by doing, thinking, looking at, hearing something different.*

These are instant one-off state modifiers. There are two ways in which the process of changing state can be deeper and longer-lasting, as well as being readily accessible and usable. These are association and dissociation, and anchoring.

Association And Dissociation

We met these concepts in the previous chapter on Visualisation. Association and dissociation are different ways of experiencing the world. When you are associated you are 'in' the experience, living it in the here and now.

Being associated is very useful if you want to enjoy pleasant experiences or memories, if you are practicing a skill or want to concentrate more intensely.

When you are dissociated, you are 'out' of the event, cut-off, out of touch. Dissociation is beneficial when reviewing an experience (e.g. your latest performance), or wishing to distance yourself from an unpleasant occurrence or memory.

We will begin by being aware of the difference between being associated and dissociated:

•*To experience being associated, sit in a chair, lean forward into a position in which you are alert, aware, poised and ready for action. Feel sensations of aliveness and vitality in your body.*

•*Bring to mind a positive and happy memory. Get right into it, looking out through your own eyes, seeing what you saw, hearing what you heard, enjoying all the happy, positive feelings you felt at the time.*

•Repeat using other positive and happy memories or experiences.

•To experience being dissociated, sit in a chair, lean back, put your hands on top of your head with your fingers interlinked, and move your head backwards. Gaze at the ceiling and allow your focus to blur. Let your body become still.

•Bring to mind an unpleasant memory. See yourself in it as if you are in a movie. Change the colour of the movie to black and white. Move the image further away, make it dimmer, less clear, softer, blurred.

•Repeat using other unpleasant memories.

What did you notice?

The unconscious mind can be friend or fiend. When you invite it to collaborate with you, it can be resourceful. By asking your unconscious mind to automatically associate and dissociate as appropriate, you will change your experience of your day-to-day life and your life overall. Ask your unconscious mind to become your ally using the sequence below:

- *I invite my unconscious mind to listen to me.*

- *I ask my unconscious mind to automatically associate into all positive memories whenever I recall them and into all positive events as I experience them.*

- *I ask my unconscious mind to automatically dissociate from unpleasant memories whenever I recall them and from all unpleasant events as I experience them.*

- *I thank my unconscious mind for listening to me.*

There are good reasons for automatically associating and dissociating.

- 'healthy' people associate into positive experiences and dissociate from negative ones;

- 'depressed' people do the reverse, dissociating from positive experiences and associating into negative ones;

- those who appear 'emotionally unstable', shifting rapidly from one state to another, tend to associate into almost all of their experiences. They feel everything with intensity;

- those who are emotionally cut off or shut down dissociate from almost all their experiences. Nothing touches them – winning a prize, being robbed or even raped, making love, ending a relationship is all much of a muchness to them. Everything is "fine" all the time.

Anchors

Anchors are triggers which are associated with a particular state. The value to the performer is that a state can be anchored so that when the trigger is fired that state is evoked. There are many examples of anchors in everyday life:

Visual anchors	Aural anchors	Kinaesthetic anchors	Olfactory anchors
Sunshine	Your name	Your favourite chair	Smell of coffee
Green traffic light	'Our' tune	A warm bath	Fresh bread
A red rose	"STOP"	Your own bed	Wine

At the trigger of a green traffic light, your foot moves from the brake to the accelerator; you turn round if someone calls your name. Phobias are examples of anchored states; a stimulus triggers a deeply-felt, uncontrollable state which was often anchored at an early age. My own phobia of birds in enclosed spaces was learned from my mother before I was 4 years old; a friend is terrified of circus clowns, a response which was almost certainly anchored during her early years. Anchors do not just exist in 'everyday' life and they have a wider currency than producing a phobic response. They can be used to invoke any desired state: to induce confidence, calmness, enthusiasm, pleasure – or any other state we choose. All that is required is that an anchor be set and, when required, triggered, and, of course that it be used and practiced.

Setting And Firing Anchors

The first step is to choose an anchor. Select one that works for you. If you are visual you might choose something relevant that you see often, for example, your instrument, an object in your rehearsal room or regular concert venue; an auditory anchor could be a word or words, such as 'Relax', 'Slow down', 'Energy'. The most commonly used kinaesthetic anchor is to squeeze a finger on your non-dominant hand with the thumb and forefinger of your dominant hand, or to touch your nose.

Whatever you choose, it should be something you can do unobtrusively as you do not want to be firing an anchor, such as standing on your head with your left foot in your mouth when on the concert platform or in an audition (unless you are auditioning to be a contortionist).

There are 5 stages to the process of setting an anchor. They are simple and straightforward, and, once you have learned the process, you can do it on your own. At first, you may wish to invite a friend or colleague to help you.

STEP 1 : ELICITING THE DESIRED STATE

In this step you get into the desired state.

Choose the desired state (e.g. confidence).

Either:

Remember a time when you were in this state (confident)

Or

Imagine that you are someone who you know or who you believe to have this desired state so that you 'model' them

Or

Take on the physical posture of the state (e.g. for confidence this might be smiling, standing upright, chest out, shoulders back, slow regular breathing)

Or

'Act as if....' (e.g. act as if you are supremely confident).

STEP 2 : GETTING INTO THE STATE

In this step you intensify the desired state as fully as you can.

Make sure that you are experiencing the state with all your senses: seeing what you would see in that state; hearing what you would hear; feeling the emotions you would feel; experiencing the bodily sensations you would have.

If necessary, intensify the state by making your experience of it nearer, brighter, louder, clearer.

STEP 3 : ANCHORING THE STATE

Choose your anchor – visual (whenever you see ....) or auditory (whenever you say or hear ....), or kinaesthetic (whenever you squeeze or touch ....)

Set the anchor.

STEP 4 : TEST THE ANCHOR

Make sure the anchor is working.

Fire the anchor and trigger the desired state.

Do you notice any difference? How do you feel?

If you notice no change, you may need to set the anchor again, or, to fire it again.

You may need to do this several times, but do not give up in despair. For some people the anchor will work first time, for others the unconscious mind may need to adjust to this new stimulus.

The more you use an anchor, the more reliable it will become. If you do not use it or boost it from time to time, it will disappear gradually. Use it or lose it!

STEP 5 : FUTURE PACE

This is to ensure that the anchor will work in a situation when you will need it.

Close your eyes and imagine a stressful situation in which you will want to use the anchor. Fire the anchor and trigger the desired state.

Do you notice a difference? If so, what is it? Describe it out loud.

If you feel it has not worked, take a break and come back to it.

If you are still feeling it has not worked, then you may need to go back to Step 1 or 2.

Chaining And Stacking Anchors

Sometimes, one anchor is not enough. Chaining anchors takes you through a sequence of states to the desired, resourceful state. This is useful where there is a large gap between your present state and the desired state; you may be so anxious before a performance that to move to a more resourceful state in which you feel calm but alert would be too great a step. In this case, move gradually from one step to the next, creating a chain of anchors by anchoring each stage with a different anchor (up your arm for example) and, then, when required, fire each anchor in turn.

State	Anchor	Where to anchor
Panic and terror	1	Wrist
Concern	2	Lower forearm
Calm	3	Middle forearm
Calm and alert	4	Upper forearm

Stacking anchors is another way of having multiple resources available to you when they are required. Decide the resources you need, anchor them using the same anchor, and then stack them one on top the other.

State	Anchor	Where to anchor
Panic and terror	1	Lower forearm
Concern	1	Lower forearm
Calm	1	Lower forearm
Calm and alert	1	Lower forearm

Changing Negative Thoughts To Positive

What you think affects how you feel, and how you feel affects how you perform. If you can change your thinking, then you can change how you perform. If negative thoughts impact adversely on the quality of your performance, and they do, positive thoughts will likewise have a beneficial influence. This exercise switches negative thoughts for positive ones and because it uses visual images, rather than anchors, I call it the Visual Switch:

- *Visualize the two situations - the 'problem' in which you have negative thoughts and the desired state in which you will have positive thoughts.*

- *Project the problem-picture into your left hand and the goal-picture into your right hand.*

- *Put your left hand about 18" in front of your face and the right hand behind you.*

- *To neutralise the problem and to replace it with the goal, move your left hand behind you and the right hand 18" in front of your face in a fast movement. If you have a friend or colleague willing to assist you, ask him or her to clap their hands to start the switch.*

- *Break state (e.g. say your full name backwards, shake*

> *your hands vigorously, jump up or down, punch the air,*
>
> *scream, etc).*
>
> • *Repeat 10 times.*

Changing Limiting Beliefs

A limiting belief is a belief which we hold about ourselves, others or the world which is general rather than specific.

"I can't play the bassoon" is not a belief about myself, but it is a statement of fact about my capability, that I do not, and have never attempted, to play the bassoon. Because it is specific, it is not a belief.

"Women can't read maps" is a belief (note: it is general, applying to all women and all maps) and it may be a limiting one if, as a male, I insist on driving with one hand and map-reading with the other while my female companion sits staring out of the window (fuming).

"I'm useless" is a limiting belief. It is a general belief which the holder will apply indiscriminately to all situations, as much to their failed attempt to make a cheese soufflé as to those areas of their life in which they have a high level of capability. The sad thing is that this belief is applied universally and replays constantly in the head. All thinking is filtered through this belief and it will be relevant and persuasive whether you are making bread, making music or making love or a glove.

There are three distinct limiting beliefs which people hold

1. I'm hopeless, I'll never do it

2. I'm helpless, I can't do it

3. I'm worthless, I don't deserve it

None of these beliefs are worth having and they can be dumped. To change a limiting belief is a liberating course of action. But, the three limiting beliefs are not the only ones which people have. Anything which comes from your past and which limits you in the present is a limiting belief:

- o "I'm ugly";
- o "I'm no good with men/women";
- o "I'm unlovable";
- o "I never play well in Newcastle / the winter / modern halls";
- o "My reeds / strings / voice always break in hot weather / Belfast / when I wear a black bra".

These are beliefs which may have served you well at some point in the past, but they are redundant in the present. Get rid of them. Now!

The approach below [22] works best if you ('Client') do it with one other person ('Facilitator') who will guide you

---

[22] Adapted from The NLP Practitioner Programme course material, © Ian McDermott (2002-3) and from Joseph O'Connor, *NLP Workbook,* 2001, p86

through the procedure, read the 'script', hold the anchors and check out how you are doing.

> 1. Identify a limiting belief – this may one of the three above, or you may have your very own, unique limiting belief!
>
> 2. Think of a time or occasion when you typically have this limiting belief and state out loud the feelings you have in this un-resourceful state.
>
> 3. Intensify and experience the state as fully as you can. The Facilitator should anchor it on your body (the left arm is a good place) and physically hold this 'negative' anchor while the Client goes back in time to when this feeling first occurred. The Facilitator checks that this is the first time, and, if the Client doesn't know when the very first time is, says "Your unconscious mind knows when this feeling first

occurred. Allow your unconscious mind to take you back to that time knowing that you will be safe".

4. Facilitator lets go of the negative anchor. Client breaks state (breathe, shake body) and the Facilitator asks the Client to come back to the present moment.

5. Ask the Client to talk about this earlier occasion and the feeling(s) they have uncovered.

6. Ask the Client to identify the resources they needed on this earlier occasion. These <u>must</u> be resources that were within their control. Write down the exact words the Client uses.

7. As the Client names these resources, anchor them in the body but in a different place from the negative one (e.g. the right arm would be an option).

8. If the Client has several resources stack the anchors (e.g.

going up the arm).

9. Facilitator physically holds the positive anchor (R). Ask the Client to go back in their mind or imagination to the original negative experience; As they do this, hold the negative anchor (L) while still holding the positive (R) and keep hold of both anchors for 10 seconds. In this way the Client has the experience of both the positive and negative state simultaneously.

10. Gently let go of the anchors. Client breaks state.

11. Now test the anchor by asking the Client to go back to the original situation and ask: "How do you feel?" "Do you notice any difference?" "What has changed?"

12. Future pace by asking the Client to imagine forwards into a situation in which they might have expected to be in an un-resourceful state. "How do you feel now?" "Do

A more gradual way of changing limiting beliefs is to use a form of auto-suggestion, known as Affirmations, which re-programme the unconscious mind. They are short statements beginning with the word "I" which overcome negative self-beliefs and increase self-esteem. These "I" statements can be about your identity ("I am ...." Or "I have ....") or your capability ("I can ....").

Affirmations:

- Always begin with the word "I", rather than "you" (which would be an affirmation about somebody else!);

- Are expressed as a positive, e.g. "I am constantly increasing my income" rather than "I am not hard up";

- Are in the present tense, because "I will" is in the future, which never comes;

- Benefit from being personalised (e.g. "I, David, love and accept myself exactly as I am");

- Should be written down where you can see them;

- Should be repeated silently or out loud in a tone of voice that tells your unconscious mind you really do believe the statement ~ your unconscious will struggle to believe that you are indeed a "happy person" if you convey the message in a dull, flat, lifeless monotone!

- Are powerful! Remember that King Midas wished for everything he touched to be turned to gold, so do be very careful what it is that you wish for ~ the unconscious can be very literal.

You should create your own affirmations, specific to your limiting beliefs, but some examples are given below to get you started:

> *"I am confident"*
>
> *"I earn good money doing what I enjoy"*
>
> *"I am creative"*
>
> *"I am successful in whatever I do"*
>
> *"I always play / sing in tune"*
>
> *"I choose health"*

Silencing Your Inner Critic

As if there are not enough critics in the world, the inner critic is one too many. This inner voice is a constituent part of us (it is by no means all of us); it is a subpersonality, a psychological satellite. When we are dominated by one or more of these constituent parts, it or they direct our lives and take us over. An analogy can be drawn with a house which has multiple occupants; different occupants coming to the fore at different times – the cook at meal times, the gardener when the lawn needs mowing, the shopper when supplies run low, the disciplinarian when other occupants step out of line, the critic when behaviour falls below expectations, the lover at moments of intimacy etc. So it is with the individual, co-existing within the same person will be a number of subpersonalities which may be in concord or conflict – the Clown, the Bitch, the Complainer, the Drunk, the Groper, the Misery, the Joker; I am sure you can draw up your own list! Performers often have a severe inner critic who comments and judges upon every performance, rehearsal and note played or sung. There is a positive intention to this Critic (as you will discover), but the long term effects of this constant criticism are as discouraging and dispiriting as if they came from a real person who followed you around 24/7, carping continuously.

Like other subpersonalities, the Critic developed originally as a defence and has now become habitual, and, it is harmful only when it controls us. It is important first to

recognise and be aware of the Critic and other
subpersonalities and then to accept them. [23]

> 1. *Consider your Critic. With your eyes closed and in a relaxed state become aware of this part of you. Let an image emerge which represents it – it may be a man or a woman, an animal, an elf, an object, yourself in disguise, a monster or anything else in the universe. Do not consciously try to find an image. Let it emerge spontaneously, as if you were watching a screen, not knowing what will shortly appear on it.*
>
> 2. *As soon as the image has appeared, give it the chance to reveal itself to you without any interference or judging on your part. Let it change if*

---

[23] The concept of Subpersonalities comes from the founder of Psychosynthesis, Roberto Assagioli (b1888-d1974) and the two exercises given here are taken from Piero Ferrucci, *What we may be*, 1982. Ferrucci collaborated closely with Dr Assagioli in Florence.

it tends to do so spontaneously, and let it show you some of its other aspects if it wants to. Get in touch with the general feeling that emanates from it.

3. *Now let this image talk and express itself. Give it space for doing so. In particular, find out what it needs. Talk with it (even if your image is an object, it can talk back to you; anything is possible in the imaginary world)! You have in front of you a subpersonality – an entity with a life and intelligence of its own.*

4. *Open your eyes and write down everything that has happened so far. Give the subpersonality a name. Write about its traits, habits and peculiarities.*

5. *You may wish to explore other subpersonalities in the same way.*

Odd though it may seem, subpersonalities carry hidden potential and "we can best facilitate this process through purposeful imagery that deliberately uses the symbolism of ascent. The imagery of climbing a mountain represents, for example, the inner act of rising to higher levels of our being, going back to the source of all life .... If we imagine climbing a mountain while carrying a particular subpersonality with us, we may be able to bring about surprising changes in it". [24] In the exercise below, you will work on your subpersonality.

> 1. *With your eyes closed and in a relaxed state, choose your subpersonality (in this case your Critic). Imagine yourself in a valley with your Critic. Together, the two of you experience your surroundings. You look around and see the grass, the*

---

[24] Ferrucci, P., *What we may be*, 1982 p 56

flowers, the trees and a mountain. Take some time

to become aware of the sounds of nature around you

– the chirping of the birds, the sounds of the leaves

in the wind, and the like.

2. *Now start walking up the mountain with your*

   subpersonality. As you keep ascending, you can

   imagine seeing all kinds of scenery, climbing

   through woods and rocks, walking on wide

   meadows or near precipices. Keep in touch with the

   increasing sense of elevation, feel the air becoming

   purer and more energising, and listen to the utter

   silence of the heights.

3. *Throughout the ascent, keep in contact with your*

   subpersonality. You may see it going through subtle

   transformations – like a variation in mood or facial

> *expression or dress – or even a radical transformation: the subpersonality changing completely into something else.*
>
> 4. *When you reach the top, let the light of the sun shine on the two of you and reveal the very essence of your subpersonality. You may see a transformation taking place once more. At this point, let the subpersonality express itself for what it is now, and let it communicate with you.*

Transforming Fearful Experiences

A life which has been lived without any trauma would be an unusual one. Most of us have experienced pain and suffering which has had a deep psychological impact – car accidents, falls, sudden illness, the death of a loved one or the end of a relationship. Not on the same scale, but psychologically as damaging are the "nightmares" we never want to happen again. I can readily think of several traumas in my life – the disappearance of a family member when I was 4 years old, the deaths of my parents, the sudden end of significant relationships, the loss of a job; all of these have left deep impressions, but there are also those which have been very stressful at the time and which continue to influence my thinking and my behaviour today – having my head held under water for too long in my first swimming lesson, my dog being run over by a motorbike, my first presentation to the Board of a bank when I was so nervous I was drenched in sweat. These are fearful experiences and they leave their mark.

The Fast Phobia Cure is a quick and effective method for overcoming trauma and the unpleasant feelings associated with it. Developed by Richard Bandler and John Grinder, the founders of NLP, in 1976, it is a synthesis of the work of hypnotist Milton Erickson and of Gestalt therapists. At that time it was called the V-K Dissociation process, as the process separates the Kinaesthetic (feeling) from the Visual stimulus that usually triggers the unconscious phobic response. The process re-educates the brain to feel comfortable with the subject or situation that caused the phobic response. I have seen this used to great and lasting effect with the survivor of a major train crash, and I have used it myself with similar results with musicians who have had traumatic performing experiences – a young pianist who went blank during a recital and was unable to recover; a singer who tripped when coming onto the platform; a brass player who fainted at the start of a solo. The practitioner does not need to know any of the detail about the incidents, thereby avoiding any of the anxiety and discomfort which might be experienced in the re-telling.

It is a process which should only be done with an experienced NLP Practitioner. Rather than describe the process so that you can do it yourself, I insist that if you suffer from phobias, traumas and Post Traumatic Stress Disorder, you seek out a NLP Practitioner who has been trained in the Fast Phobia Cure (or the Rewind Technique as it is also known). Such a Practitioner should:

• Relax you first – this usually involves guided imagery or hypnosis;

• Make you feel comfortable;

• Avoid referring to upsetting incidents in too much detail;

• Have adequate training in both relaxation skills and the Fast Phobia Cure itself (having read a book about it is inadequate);

• Be able to demonstrate prior success with the technique;

• Help you there and then – one session is normally sufficient (but be aware that, while benefits will be felt immediately, it may be some weeks before the mind and body are completely healed).

The case study below describes the process I used with the young lady who had 'blanked' during her piano recital:

Sophie is 27. She trained at one of the UK's leading conservatoires and with professors in England and Europe. At the time of the trauma, she was in the midst of a recital tour in Europe, one objective of which was to promote her recently released CD of a particular composer's piano works.

What bothered her the most from her experience was the moment at which she blanked and stopped playing. Not only did she feel as though she had lost her mind and her bodily functioning, she remembered hearing a long silence and then a gasp from the audience. On a scale of trauma,

---

she rated it at 10 (extremely disturbing).

STAGE 1: I asked Sophie to imagine that she was in a small cinema looking at a blank screen. I asked her to see an image of herself on the screen in black & white without any sound. Next I suggested she imagine herself in the projection booth of the cinema watching herself in the audience observing the image of herself on the screen. These are important steps: first, seeing the image in black & white without any sound reduces the intensity of the experience. By moving into the projection booth, this adds distance and reduces the intensity of the experience as Sophie is observing Sophie watching an image of herself. In Sophie's case this was not enough as she still felt extremely fearful and began again to experience some of the physical and mental rigidity she had felt at the time of the trauma.

So, I recommended that she insert a thick sheet of transparent plastic between herself in the booth and herself in the auditorium and another between herself in her seat in the cinema and the screen. Further by making this screen bullet proof and 'smoked' (i.e. instead of being clear plastic, it was changed into smoky brown. This created more distance between Sophie and the silent, black and white image on the screen).

Sophie now reviewed her performance, dissociated, watching herself from the projection booth, watching herself in the audience, seeing the black & white, silent film. I asked her to watch the film until she reached the point when the event was over and she knew that she was safe again, and then to stop the film and make a still image of herself at the point when she was safe again. This was *the first time she had been able to think about the performance without being physically and mentally overwhelmed with fear. Progress!*

STAGE 2: The next stage was to ask Sophie to imagine herself leaving the projection booth and going and sitting in her seat in the cinema. I then invited her to walk up to the cinema screen and step into the still image at the point at which she felt safe. I requested that she rewind the scene back to the point just before the trauma occurred in about 5 seconds and that she repeat this several times, each time getting faster; the final couple of times, I asked her to rewind it in the time it took me to clap my hands. This is like watching a videotape rewinding and it has the effect of re-imprinting the traumatic memory in a different way (backwards) – it scrambles the information that was imprinted at the time of the trauma; in this new form it no longer makes sense and loses its power. Finally, Sophie stood up, shook her arms and body and took a deep breath.

What had changed? Sophie rated the intensity of the traumatic memory as having dropped from 10 to 5. She had re-imprinted the way her mind had encoded the trauma. She had changed from seeing herself as though it was happening to her again in the here and now, to remembering the scene as though it was of someone else that she was watching in a video and, as a result, her representation of this was more muted – the colours were duller, the sounds more indistinct. This indicates that Sophie has lowered the intensity of the event and is becoming de-sensitised to it. It is losing its influence and

> *her grip on her.*
>
> *I next spoke to Sophie when she called me for a "check-in" call some weeks later and she reported a further reduction in the intensity to "around 3, maybe 2".*

This case study of Sophie demonstrates the use of the Fast Phobia Cure to alleviate the trauma associated with a single incident. Not all traumas are single events, some are cumulative, for example repeated occurrences of 'blanking'; in such cases, it is important to work on each incident and every important aspect of each incident to achieve complete desensitization and alleviation of the symptoms of the trauma.

3. PRACTICE AND PERFORMANCE

The Art Of Practice [25]

To be effective, practice needs to be as well considered as performance. As a professional musician, it is likely that you have discarded the approach to practice that you had as a child ~ practicing scales while eating a peanut butter sandwich, watching TV, pinching your sister, and daydreaming about the heart-throb on the school bus!

The performance itself is one part of a long process. If you are giving an instrumental recital with another musician, it might look as follows:

---

[25] The approach and strategies proposed in this chapter are based on my work with individual clients and [l] on work with students who participated in the *Zoning-In* project at the Royal College of Music, London and [2] on Part II, *Practice Strategies* in Williamon, A., *Musical Excellence*, Oxford University Press, 2004

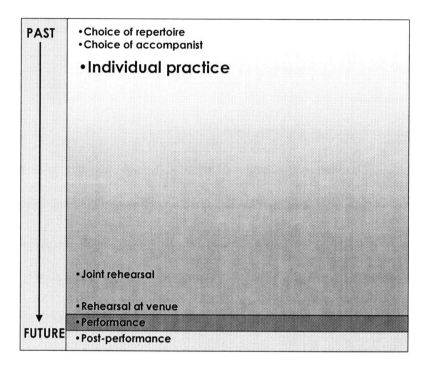

This puts the performance in a wider context and to see it like this, visually, reveals the small amount of time actually taken up by the performance itself. Most of the time – in theory! – is spent practicing. Peak performance involves peak practice.

There are two tasks to be undertaken before even the first note is played or sung in practice:

    1. Preparing and organising;

144

2. Time management or the frequency and duration of practice.

1. Preparing And Organising Practice

To prepare for practice, ask yourself the following questions:

> *How do I warm up for practice? Is it just a habit? What could I do differently that would be more effective?*
>
> *What is my practice routine? Do I do the same things in the same order? What can I do to make it more interesting and effective and to keep it fresh?*
>
> *If I have no routine, what would be the benefits of having one?*
>
> *Do I always focus on rehearsing new pieces? Would there be any benefit in mixing in some old repertoire?*

Planned practice has been shown to be more effective. Going back to your schooldays, you probably recall that practice consisted of sidling disdainfully up to your instrument, opening the score, staring at it in uncomprehending disbelief, picking at the easier bits and filling in any remaining time by examining the bits of your anatomy that nowadays you probably only get to see in the mirror (if then). As a strategy this probably worked, if it carried you through Grade 8, the music academy of your choice and a glittering solo or ensemble career. How much more stellar might that career have been (or be) if you had a strategy? Here is one to try:

A. *Plan what to do*

B. *Know why you are doing it*

C. *Know what you wish to accomplish*

Imagine that the repertoire for a performance in three month's time includes:

1. Mozart (3 movements, standard repertoire, many previous performances);
2. Beethoven (3 movements, out of repertoire for a couple of years);
3. Rachmaninov (20 sections, most of them in repertoire, but two sections – XIV and XX – are rusty);
4. Finzi (two previous performances, one of them disastrous, but piece requested by sponsor of the concert);
5. *Vision de Les Dawson* (21st century commission from a Rochdale *enfant terrible*, first performance, unreadable score, staggeringly difficult number of notes, no time or key signatures, unconventional notation, requires synchronisation with obscure tapes interweaving Indian birdsong, Gracie Fields and Ghanaian dance rhythms).

A.   Plan What To Do

This repertoire is a big chunk to learn, so "chunk down" by making the big chunks smaller, and then make them smaller still.

A big-chunk goal would be to "learn the repertoire" and, if that isn't big enough, throw in "from memory" as well! Yes, yes, of course, of course, that is the ultimate goal, but it is just too big. This is where "planning what to do" comes in.

You have 12 weeks, 5 working days per week plus other commitments: family, pupils, ex-spouse's wedding in Dorking and a celebrity golf tournament in Spain.

This is how your goals and plan might look:

Day	Week			
	1	2	3	4
M	Mozart	Beethoven	Rachmaninov	Etc
T	Beethoven	Rachmaninov	Finzi	
W	Rachmaninov	Finzi	Commission	
T	Finzi	Commission	Mozart	
F	Commission	Mozart	Beethoven	

Even this is too big a chunk. Chunk down into smaller chunks. You have 60 days and can afford, say, 4 hours a day to practice. Plan the 60 days by the hour or half hour if necessary:

Time	Day		etc
	Monday	Tuesday	
0900 – 1000 [60']	Commission p1 Mozart 1st Mov	Commission p2+3 Rachmaninov section XX (new) Mozart 3rd Mov	
1000 – 1030	Break	Break	
1030 – 1130 [60']	Commission p2 Beethoven 2nd Mov	Commission p4 Finzi Moto perpetuo	
1130 - 1200	Break	Break	
1200-1300 [60']	Commission p1+2 Rachmaninov section XIV (new)	Rachmaninov XIV and XX Beethoven 3rd Mov	
1300-1400	Lunch	Lunch	
1400-1500 [60']	Commission p3 Finzi Presto	Commission p5 Commission p1-4 Rachmaninov I-X	

This schedule has a number of essential constituents:

- Variety overall and within the 60 minute slots;

- A combination of the familiar and the new; but even when working on the familiar Mozart, resist the temptation to rattle it off in uncritical autopilot. Keep it fresh, play it faster, play it real slow, play it like Barenboim, Dame Myra Hess, Mrs Mills, Jools Holland! Or, why not, play it like Mozart?

- The day always ends on a 'high' with something which is familiar. It would be ill-advised to end the day note-bashing your way through the whole of the commissioned piece (Gracie and all);

- Regular breaks. Take them. Set an alarm clock if need be. Stand up, walk around, leave the room, have tea or coffee, talk to someone, go outside.

B. *Know Why You Are Doing It*

It is obvious that you are practicing these pieces because you have to perform them in three months time. That is a good enough reason in itself, but, again, the chunk is too big. Chunk the reason down!

Why are you practicing page 1 of the commission? What is your goal? Is it to learn the notes? Are you practicing technical or expressive aspects of the piece? Be as precise as you can - is it intonation, bowing, rhythm, rhythmic accuracy?

C.   *Know What You Wish To Accomplish*

"A man without a goal is like a ship without a rudder" (Thomas Carlyle). Your schedule will help with this. You have set aside time to work on page 1 of the commission and this may be what you wish to accomplish, but it is not very precise and you may come away feeling as though you have achieved very little. If you set yourself a goal – "I will master the notes on page 1, mark any that are uncertain, pencil in fingering / breathing etc, and play the page through twice at the correct tempo" – you will be able to say and will feel as though you have achieved something worthwhile. As you progress, the goal will change.

2. Time Management

The practice schedule is part of time management, but there are two other, related issues to consider – the frequency and duration of practice.

In working with students at the Royal College of Music, I discovered early on that practicing, even for the gifted, is a chore, something that has to be done, and that not practicing usually has penalties attached to it (the wrath of the professor being a short term one). It was clear that (a) practicing is not regarded as fun and (b) the students were "big chunk" practicers. A dialogue might be as follows:

David   "What have you done this week?"

Student   "Monday, I practiced"

David   "All day?"

Student   "Yeah. I got up, came to college, started about 9.30 and then went home about 6"

David	"And you spent that time practicing?"
Student	"Yeah"
David	"All of it?"
Student	"Yeah .... Well, I went a bit dreamy at times and my mind wandered, and I went to the loo. I didn't feel to have achieved much"

I bet!! Eight hours so-called practicing is enough to make anyone go a bit dreamy. Apart from issues about blood-sugar levels due to the lack of food, dehydration, the single visit to the loo, how effective is this sort of approach? How much of that time is productive? I would bet a Steinway grand and a Stradivarius that a speeded-up video recording of the 8 hour marathon would reveal two things – that most of the time was wasted, and that the peak occurred sometime during the first hour. It is highly likely that this student could have spent 6 hours with friends, watching TV or sleeping in the library and have achieved just as much, if not more.

Is practicing one day a week for 7 hours, preferable to practicing 7 days a week for an hour a day? That is for you to decide, but studies of learning show that regular practice (e.g. daily) and for short periods of time is the more effective.

Eight hours, six hours, four hours in a single lump is probably more than the body and mind can comfortably manage. We have this heroic image of the committed musician passed down to us from black-and-white movies: a 19th century consumptive virtuoso is hunched coughing over his instrument (always a him; the her is a pale-faced beauty with an alluring embonpoint lying invitingly atop an unmade bed), a scrap of bread on a pewter plate, icicles hanging from the window – and all of this in the name of his noble, tortured calling. This approach may work for one in a million, but I doubt you are that one!

In the sample schedule above, no practice session was longer than 60 minutes and there are breaks of ½ hour after each hour of practice with an hour for lunch. The chunks are small and manageable, and there is time for re-fresh-ment. The likelihood of becoming fatigued or bored is minimised and the chances of actually achieving something concrete and positive are enhanced.

Routines

So what do you do before a performance? It is advantageous to know this and to know what works for you and what doesn't.

Take three scenarios:

1. You leave home late after a row with him or her indoors, you miss the train, you have trouble finding the concert venue, you arrive flustered for the rehearsal, realise you have left your reading glasses in the mother-in-law's loo, you have a momentary memory lapse early in your first piece, and everything then goes rapidly downhill. Just how much worse can it get? In the time between rehearsal and concert you are so strung up

that you cannot eat or drink, your stomach is churning and you feel sick. When you go on stage you are so uptight you just know that you will screw up .... and you do!

2. You have a lazy day with friends, you fall deeply asleep in the train going to the concert, you arrive feeling disconnected, half asleep and very relaxed; you feel as though nothing could possibly go wrong and even if it does, heigh-ho, tomorrow is another day. Nothing does go wrong, but you feel as if your performance lacks edge and the audience reaction is, to say the least, muted.

3. You sleep well the night before the concert, get up and do some very focused practice of the tricky passages, you go for a vigorous walk by the river, read a book on the train, feel stimulated by the rehearsal in which you

feel there is a spiritual connection between yourself and the other players. Just before the performance you warm up by doing your relaxation exercises and some mental rehearsal. You feel confident and alert, but also relaxed. The performance is a dream, you are floating, it is as if you produce magic by doing nothing, but, at the same time, you are aware of being fully in control of your performing state.

A successful performance requires planning and will be infinitely more successful than a "What-the-hell–it'll-be-alright-on-the-night" approach. The planning is part of the process of warming up for the performance to come. Warming up is vital: if you watch footballers coming on to the pitch and waiting for the whistle to blow, they spend the time warming up; if you watch tennis from Wimbledon, players will engage in a routine before they hit the first ball. In fact, the warm up will have started before they come onto the pitch or the court – it may start as they begin the day, or even days or weeks before.

I recommend a four stage approach to a performance:

1. Mental preparation;

2. The week before the performance;

3. The day of the performance;

4. At the venue.

1. Mental Preparation

What do you do in preparation for the up-coming performance you have? You have been practicing for months or weeks (following the schedule you devised in the previous chapter) and the performance is imminent. Sure, you could keep on practicing right up until the moment you step out on to the stage, but, while you do need to be technically and musically prepared, there is some additional preparation you can do mentally which has the capacity to transform a routine performance into an exciting one. This mental preparation should begin in the week or so before you go onto the platform.

At Findhorn, a spiritual community in the north-east of Scotland, every activity begins with an attunement, or an 'at-one-ment'; another form of warming up. It is a short silence during which the individual or group focuses on the here-and-now, allowing the perspective to shift from outside concerns and demands to the inner self and the task at hand. Before practice or performance, this moment of silence allows you to tune in to yourself; if you are practicing in or performing with a group it gives you time to tune in to yourself and to others in the group.

You can heighten the quality of your practice and your performance by following the simple warm up routine below:

❏ *Warm up physically: this might involve some breathing, some gentle stretching, some neck or back exercises, but nothing too strenuous. Use one of the relaxation techniques described earlier to relax both your mind and your body. If you feel too relaxed, do something to change your state, either by anchoring a higher state of arousal or by doing something physical – fast breathing or jumping up and down.*

❏ *Warm up mentally: spend time building your confidence by using mental rehearsal, replaying your peak performances or saying affirmations. Focus only and always on the positive and feel this flowing through your body until you are full of confidence and the unshakable belief that you will perform at your very best.*

- *Warm up spiritually: use the attunement approach described above to become centred within and at one with yourself and the other players. You might do this on your own or as a group. If attuning with a group, this may be an uncomfortable experience at first for some members, but they will become accustomed to it. An ensemble group I worked with experienced some level of discomfort and embarrassment initially, but now incorporate a group attunement as an essential part of their warm up routine.*

- *Warm up instrumentally: this might include some technical exercises or anything which reconnects you to your instrument. In his novel* **An Equal Music,** *Vikram Seth has the string quartet in which the hero*

> *plays begin their rehearsals by playing a four octave*
>
> *scale in unison; this brings them together as a group as*
>
> *well as focusing them on their instruments.*

You can also prepare mentally for your performance, by mentally rehearsing the concert in advance:

> ❑ *Sit comfortably in a chair with your whole body well*
> *supported. Breathe in and out several times: IN 2, 3, 4;*
> *HOLD, 2; OUT 2, 3, 4, 5, 6; PAUSE, 2. Repeat three*
> *times.*
>
> ❑ *Allow your body to relax further into the chair with*
> *each out-breath.*
>
> ❑ *Your instrument is your ally, you need it on your side*
> *and working for you.*
>
>   o *If you have a portable instrument, such as a*

violin or trumpet, imagine yourself making friends with it, see and hear yourself talking to it in whatever way is appropriate.

- o *If you are a vocalist, imagine talking to your vocal chords and respiratory system.*

- o *If you are a pianist or organist, imagine yourself walking up to your instrument, touching it, befriending it.*

❑ *See yourself walking on to the platform. Notice what you are wearing, how you are walking, your body posture. Imagine a slight smile of pleasure on your face and notice how relaxed but alert you feel. You are feeling at your very best, you are at your peak.*

❑ *Observe yourself beginning to play in the perfect performance. Everything is perfect − tuning, articulation, expression, dynamic control.... all of them are perfect. Follow the performance through to its conclusion.*

□ *Finally, hear and feel the applause and adulation. This has been the perfect performance, experience it in your body, know it in your mind, feel it in your emotions.*

□ *Allow the scene to fade and come back into the room. Enjoy the positive, warm feelings it gives you. Become aware of the relaxed feeling you have in your body, the calm feeling in your mind and your emotions.*

□ *Go play!*

If there is a particular state you want to be in when you practice or perform, there is another form of anchoring known as The Circle Of Excellence, which, when working with children, I call "The Magic Circle", for the quite simple reason that it has magical results!

1. *Draw a circle on the floor in your imagination.*

2. *Choose up to three qualities that you want to have access to generally or for a specific situation.*

3. *Go back in your memory to a time when you had the first quality.*

4. *With your eyes closed, relive that moment ~ seeing what you saw, hearing what you heard, and feeling what you felt.*

5. *Allow this to build in intensity by making it bigger, clearer, brighter, sharper, louder.*

6. *When the quality is at its most intense, step into the circle and anchor it physically or with a word.*

7. *Step out of the circle, leaving that quality inside the*

circle. Break your state by dancing a little jig, saying your phone number backwards, or stretching.

8. Repeat for the second and third qualities using steps 3 to 7.

9. You have now anchored all three qualities and are standing outside the circle. Break state. Step back into the circle, close your eyes, and feel yourself filled with these three qualities. Enjoy the experience. Be aware of the confidence and the positive feelings you now have available to you.

10. Finally, test it by thinking of a time or situation when you will need these qualities. Imagine the scene ~ where, when, who will be there etc. Notice how you feel. Do you feel different? In what way?

Before a performance, draw the circle in your imagination in the area where you are going to stand or sit when on stage, and consciously step into the circle as you go on to perform.

There is an alternative to this known as A Piece Of Cake. For this I am indebted to Tim Hallbom and Suzi Smith[26], renowned NLP practitioners and trainers. It has the joy of being simple and effective.

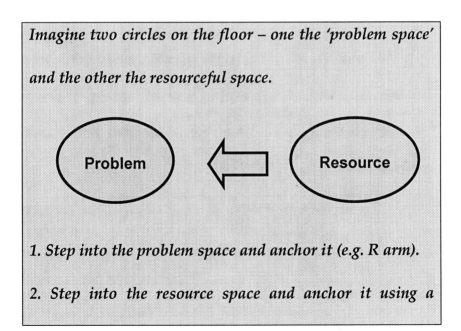

Imagine two circles on the floor – one the 'problem space' and the other the resourceful space.

1. Step into the problem space and anchor it (e.g. R arm).

2. Step into the resource space and anchor it using a

---

[26] This technique has been adapted from The NLP Master Practitioner Programme, ITS, 2003

different part of your body (e.g. L arm).

3. Holding the physiology of the resource space (i.e. your posture, your breathing, plus the feelings you have), step into the problem space.

4. Finally, test the resource which you have just transferred to make sure it will work in all the contexts in which you may need it.

Imprinting a past peak performance on your unconscious mind is a powerful way of making available the positive thoughts and feelings associated with a past experience [27].

Think back and find an exceptional time in your life, a time when you experienced a peak performance, a

---

[27] This is an adaptation of Richard Bandler's *Decision Destroyer* as devised by Steve Andreas and Charles Faulkner; they call it "Creating a peak performance imprint" and I have adapted it further specifically for performing musicians. See Andreas, S., and Faulkner, C., *NLP The New Technology of Achievement,* Nicholas Brealey Publishing, 1994

time when you were "in the zone". Step back into it and

see what you saw, hear what you heard, feel what you felt

and experience it as if it is happening again now.

Now think of an ordinary, unexceptional memory –

a phone call, going into a shop.

Notice the differences between the sights, sounds

and feelings of the exceptional experience and imagine you

are going to make a movie of it. Notice its cinematic

qualities: its location, size, richness of visual, auditory

details etc and make a quick inventory of these. This is

your brain's special way of coding this time in your life

when you performed so well.

Make this memory of your peak performance

bigger, bolder, brighter, more real, sharper, more clear.

Imagine floating out of your body with this

resource and going back along your timeline into your past. As you float, ask yourself where in your past the possession of this resource would have made a tremendous difference. Find one, and when you do, come down on your timeline at a point before *you needed this resource.*

Now, quickly travel forward through time, noticing how this incredible resource transforms your past memories into exceptionally resourceful ones. When you reach the present, watch yourself with this resource travelling on into your future.

You now have three ways of improving your performance – The Circle Of Excellence, A Piece Of Cake and The Peak Performance Imprint. What a treasure house of riches you can draw upon to give exceptional performances!

2. The Week Before The Performance

During the course of the final week, you will be putting a lot of time and energy into mastering the music and it may be tempting to do this to the exclusion of all else. You will need breaks, and will need to do something other than music-making to achieve contrast and, hence, balance in your life. Some of this time can be spent planning non-musical aspects of performance, which can be loosely described as the who, where, when, how and what:

> ❑ *Who are you performing with? Have you had confirmation of this? Is there anything you need to check? Any information missing? Do you need to know*

who is playing the cow bells etc?

- *Where is the performance – precisely. To know it is in Glasgow may not be enough information. What is the address, postcode, phone number? Who at the venue is co-ordinating the performance?*

- *When is the performance? Date, time? What time is the rehearsal and where?*

- *How will you get there? How long will it take? How long will you be away? Do you need to book train or air tickets, or an hotel?*

- *What will you wear for the performance? Is it clean, washed, ironed etc? Do you have spare items of clothing? Do you have cufflinks, jewellery? Do you have spare glasses / contact lenses? What about toothbrush, make up? What will you wear before and* after the performance? If you are staying overnight, what else will you need? Do you have something to read or music to listen to on your iPod, MP3?

❏ What will you eat in the days before performance? On the day of the performance itself?

❏ What will be your sleeping routine? Will you aim to be in bed by a certain time each night during the week before?

❏ How will you practice in the week before? Clearly you will be aiming to replicate in practice the performance that you aim to give, so you will be concentrating on accurate and expressive rehearsal. If you make a mistake, do NOT stop, keep playing just as you would in performance; you can go back and correct it later, but, for the moment, let it go.

3.   The Day Of The Performance

The day itself has arrived. Your focus will be on you and the forthcoming performance ~ you could do with a high dosage of positivity and optimism (which is not an eye complaint!).

> ❑ *Begin the day by thinking positively. You may want to start with some relaxation, some affirmations and a short mental rehearsal of yourself arriving at the venue and giving the perfect, faultless performance.*
>
> ❑ *Take time to prepare yourself, shower or bathe slowly and pleasurably. Use your favourite lotions and potions, dress slowly and carefully, admire yourself once you are ready and tell yourself how good you feel.*
>
> ❑ *Decide what you are going to eat and when you are going to eat it. Eat light foods, resist the allure of*

caffeine and other stimulants (especially alcohol, so if this is a part of your daily life, promise yourself a good couple of drinks after the performance).

❑ *Make sure you have all you need for the day – your clothes, instrument, music, food, water, pills, book, spectacles, overnight clothing etc.*

❑ *Do whatever you need to do in any spare time to be at maximum positivity – prepare yourself mentally and physically. Meditate, walk slowly somewhere quiet, breathe in the breath of life and of tranquillity. Mentally rehearse all of your pieces, imagine yourself walking onto the platform, see yourself filled with confidence, do any technical exercises which will help you.*

4.   At The Venue

You're there! In this final stage, there are still things to do:

> □ *Get to know the venue. Where are the other players, the entrances and exits, fire escapes, toilets, food, drink.*
>
> □ *What, if anything is likely to distract you? Can anything be done about this? Who do you need to speak to about it?*
>
> □ *Where will you be standing, sitting? If you need a chair, is one provided? A music stand?*
>
> □ *Go through your physical and mental warm up. Do another mental rehearsal of your pieces, ensuring that this rehearsal is as perfect as it possibly can be. Do any affirmations that you think would be helpful. Be extremely positive.*
>
> □ *Make sure you have laid down your Circle of*

> *Excellence.*
>
> ❏ *Finally, surround yourself in a magical circle of golden light shining down on you from above and ask that light to guard you, guide you and protect you during the performance.*

You should be adequately hydrated by drinking water, although there are two caveats to this:

1. Don't drink so much that you spend most of the performance wanting to go to the lavatory;

2. If you are a singer, water tends to dry out the vocal cords, so instead, eat slices of apple to stimulate the flow of mucus.

Have your 'final' meal well in advance of the performance and keep it light (pasta is ideal, but resist the sauce made of 48 different cheeses!). After that, eat light food – bananas and rice cakes are highly recommended as they fill the gaps without being heavy.

Chapter 10
Performance

Concentration And Focus

The performance itself is the thing that you have been building up to. There is nothing – repeat: nothing – that is more important at this moment. Your total focus must be on the performance and distractions must be cast aside.

I am grateful to John Syer and Christopher Connolly[28] for introducing me to their "Black Box" technique. They developed the "technique with Barbara Lynch, who subsequently won the 1979 European Trap-Shooting title. There are innumerable distractions that can occur between shooting and preparing for the next shot". So their approach has pedigree and considerable relevance, particularly for orchestral musicians and concerto soloists who can also be subject to innumerable

---

[28] Syer, J., and Connolly, C., *Sporting Body, Sporting Mind: An Athlete's Guide to Mental Training,* Simon & Schuster Ltd, 1987, pp 14-15

distractions between 'shots'! But it has application also when preparing to go on to the platform in enabling the performer to put aside minor niggles and major disturbances.

Having identified your concerns and distractions, sit quietly, close your eyes, take a deep breath and allow yourself to settle heavily into your chair as you breathe out slowly.

Imagine yourself sitting at a desk in front of a window. Look out and notice what you see, what the weather is like, what movement there may be. Then look down at the desk and notice a blank sheet of paper and a pen. Pick up the pen and write down a complete list of those distractions and concerns you identified. As you write, see the shape of your handwriting on the page, hear the point of your pen slide over the paper, feel the weight of your upper body on your arm. If you find it easier you can draw

a picture to represent the distractions or your distracted

mood.

When you have finished put down the pen, fold up the piece

of paper and turn around. You see a box behind you,

somewhere within reach. It may be on a shelf or on the

floor. Notice how large it is, what colour it is and whether

it is in the light or the shadow. Open the lid. Then put the

folded piece of paper inside the box, close the lid and turn

back to the desk, settling back into your chair and once

more looking out of the window.

Having done this, you can open your eyes.

However, it is important that once your performance is

over, you again close your eyes and go back to this

imaginary desk, turn around, open the box, get out and

> *unfold the piece of paper and look to see what you wrote or drew. Sometimes this will no longer be of interest and that's fine but, if the exercise is to continue to work – and with time it can become increasingly effective – the part of you that has been promised attention later on must learn to trust that it will get that attention.*

One of the fears of every performer is loss of concentration during performance. My sister in law, now in her 60s, was, when younger, a promising violinist. By the time this uninhibited, bohemian and passionate girl came into the life of our conventional family at the age of 18, she had given up the instrument and would never play it again. A few years earlier she had been playing in a concert in her home town of Bedford. It was a 1950s charity 'do' attended by the great and good of the town, dressed in their finest for an evening of what many of them must have regarded as a painful duty. In the third or fourth row was a large female dignitary dressed in a fur coat and atop her tightly coiffed hair was a pillar-box red felt hat decorated with a long and waving feather. Helena, playing from music, caught sight of this avarian adornment at the end of each stave. For the first page or so she resisted the temptation to dwell on the feather, but finally it got her. She fixed on the feather and her performance came to a halt. She never recovered ..... and she never played again. She was so humiliated by her poor performance that she gave up on years of violin lessons, many hours of practice and her ambition of being a great soloist.

This is an example of a catastrophic loss of concentration and most performers will not experience this even once in their life. More likely is it that you will experience momentary lapses of concentration which may throw you off balance. Concentration is a perfect but achievable state where your focus is totally and exclusively on what you are doing at the time. You are associated and fully in the present moment.

We in the West do seem to find it particularly difficult to live in the present moment; in fact, most of us probably divide our time between the past and the future in almost equal measure, coming into the present for a millisecond only at peak moments. The perfect performance state is one of being fully in the present, free, involved, responsive and aware.

If you watch someone who is in this state, they change physically. When Ken, my best friend at school and an excellent pianist, was in his ideal performance state, his face would become expressionless, almost mask-like, he would go pale and his mouth would drop open. 'Why do you play with your mouth open?' I asked. 'Didn't know I did' was his curt reply. My father, when concentrating during a golf swing, would stick his tongue out about half an inch; when he did this, I knew that he would hit a good shot.

Concentration is important, but you do not need to concentrate at this high level of intensity all the time (even if you could). It is handy to know how to bring yourself into this powerful state and the key to this is awareness. In the procedure described below you will be enabled to shift your focus from one which is loose (e.g. broad and directed externally) to one which is tight (e.g. narrow and focused internally). A violin soloist client of mine says that when he is about to play and requires 100% concentration, he narrows his focus to his instrument and pays meticulous attention to what his hands are doing, the feel of the string against his fingers, the colour of his instrument; in other words he brings himself right in and up close and focuses on something external, his instrument. This works for him; your approach may be different.

The sport psychologist, Robert Nideffer, [29] distinguished between different types of attention which he

---

[29] Nideffer, R., *Psyched to Win,* Leisure Press, 1992.

defined by width - broad or narrow - and direction - internal or external:

- Narrow Internal: The focus is directed inwards and you will be paying attention to your own feelings, emotions and physical sensations.

- Narrow External: Your attention will be on a narrow range of things outside of yourself e.g. looking at your fingers, watching the conductor, listening to the instrumentalist whose entry marks the approach of your own, listening to the sound you are producing.

- Broad Internal: Your attention will be on a wide range of feelings, emotions, physical sensations inside yourself. This is experienced when you are mentally rehearsing (or worrying about) your forthcoming performance – be it a 2 second blast on the trombone, or a whole concerto.

• Broad External: Your focus is on a broad range of things outside of yourself e.g what the rest of the ensemble is doing or playing, what is going on in the audience.

You cannot do all these things or be in all these attentional places at once, so you develop the capability of moving from one to the other as appropriate. The problem for most performers is that they get stuck in a particular focus at the wrong time. The challenge is to be able to shift easily and at will between the four different states. This requires practice, shifting from quickly from one state to another, and you can try this sitting in a chair at home:

> ❑ *Narrow internal: notice exactly what you are thinking now, precisely what you are feeling emotionally now, be aware of any specific sensations in your body now,*

any images you have now.

- *Move quickly on to ....*

- *Broad internal: pay attention to your wider thoughts, feelings and bodily sensations.*

- *Move quickly on to ....*

- *Narrow external: focus on any sounds inside the room, feel the chair you are sitting on (is it hard or soft, where does it support you?), concentrate closely on an object near to hand (the floor, the carpet, a light fitting).*

- *Move quickly on to ....*

- *Broad external: listen for sounds outside of the room, look out of the window and observe what you can see. Move as far out into the external world as you can, noticing sounds that are far away, seeing objects that are in the distance.*

> ❏ *And now, move between these states in random order, saying to youself (e.g.) narrow internal, broad external, broad internal, narrow external, broad external etc. Repeat this for 5 minutes.*
>
> ❏ *Finally, wherever you have ended up, find a position which is balanced between all four states where you are aware of both internal and external, broad and narrow – this is your centre.*

Managing Mistakes

This is a taboo area for professional musicians and it is remarkable that books on music performance seldom refer to this critical aspect. It is, after all, unrealistic to expect to make no mistakes. They are a fact of performing life and anybody who imagines that they will be able to turn in performance after performance without making a single gaffe is likely to be seriously disappointed. As a goal, a clanger-free performance is indeed desirable and achievable. How a blunder affects you will depend upon (a) your perception of what a lapse is and isn't; (b) the language you use to describe a blunder; and (c) your ability to deal with a slip-up when it happens, whether it be before, during or after performance. Once the event has passed, you have the opportunity to review what happened and to reframe your experience.

Lapse Perception

You know that you have made a mistake. Let's say you played or sang a wrong note, or, you came in a beat too early or a beat too late, or, you held a note for too long or not long enough. Just how serious is this? How serious is it in the context of the whole piece, the total concert? You may feel dreadful, but the audience may not even notice.

In the mid-1970s I went to hear Michael Roll play the Beethoven 4th Piano Concerto in Leeds Town Hall. It was a charity event and the prominent citizens of Leeds were packed into the gallery in DJs and evening glad rags. Roll had been a pupil of Fanny Waterman and the very first prize-winner of the Leeds International Pianoforte Competition in 1963. He was home-grown talent and the Jewish community of Leeds was out in force to support their 'boy'.

The first movement opens, unusually and famously, with the piano soloist playing simple chords in the tonic key before modulating to the dominant; the orchestra then enters. Roll came on to the platform, sat at the piano, paused ... and paused ..... and paused. He stood up apologised to the audience and left the stage, but what he had said was drowned out by the collective gasp of horror from the gallery. Behind me, an elderly matron exclaimed "Poor Mrs Roll"! If this sample of one is a yardstick, the audience's sympathies and concerns were with the pianist's mother, not the pianist. Roll returned to the platform and gave a flawless performance.

Has it ruined his career? No - he has since recorded the complete Beethoven concerti with the RPO and Howard Shelley and his agent's website is testimony to his success.

Does he even remember it? Probably, and if he does, I guess he laughs about it now. Did it matter? No.

Mistakes are to be avoided and minimised, but performers need to be aware of over-reacting to minor flaws and blemishes – and to major ones too.

The Language Of Lapses

How do you define a mistake? What word do you use? Write it down now in CAPITAL letters in the centre of a piece of paper and then round it write all the other words you know of which you could use to describe a mistake.

You might have written down some of the words in the first paragraph of this section – mistake, blunder, gaffe, clanger, lapse, blemish, slip-up – and there are plenty more: error, fault, boob, fault, slip, flaw, inaccuracy, oversight, bloomer, faux pas, muddle, boo-boo, miscalculation, etc.

Now, on another sheet of paper, take all these words, yours and mine, and rank them in order of their gravity: is a slip-up more serious than a slip? Or a boob more grave than a boo-boo? You decide.

If at the top of your list, you have 'clanger' and at the bottom 'boo-boo' and your word in capital letters was MISTAKE and this now sits in the middle of your list, you can begin to change the language you use to describe your mistakes. Then you no longer have one universal word to cover all errors, but a wide and differentiated vocabulary to employ.

For example, you are singing in a concert and you forget the words of the song you are singing – most singers would class this at the catastrophic end of mistake-making and you might elect to call it a clanger. On the other hand, if you sing or play a B flat instead of B natural, this might be at the low end of the scale of disaster and you may describe it as a slip or boo-boo. It is all a matter of the language you use and the terminology of the people who have taught you.

Teachers, along with parents, have to shoulder much of the burden for how we view ourselves. Many is the time I have heard from otherwise intelligent and capable adults that they gave up the piano / violin / recorder because their teacher said they were useless or stupid. A bassoonist told me that his teacher once said "You are both a genius and a fool. Your playing is so full of foolish mistakes that you have the genius to rewrite the whole piece". This is scarcely encouraging.

Re-programme your mind so that it codes inaccuracies in a different way, using different words and you may find that you make far fewer mistakes!

Dealing With Mistakes

If you have looked at the way in which you perceive lapses and the language you use, you are well on your way to dealing with them. That said, there is always more you can do. There are three further issues:

1. Before you perform - how to minimise mistakes and to prepare your own 'rescue strategy';

2. During performance – how to deal with a mistake at the time;

3. After – how to learn from it.

1. Before Performance

Mistakes which occur during practice have to be unlearned, so find a practicing strategy that works for you and which minimises mistakes, being sure to   resolve problems rather than hope they will go away, because they won't.

A practicing strategy which aimed to minimise mistakes could be to chunk up or to chunk down:

- Play through the entire piece several times (chunking up).
- Play parts of it, then bring it together (chunking down and then up).
- Play the whole and then practice the parts (chunking up then down).

Where a piece has difficult or challenging passages, choose technical exercises relevant to the problem and reassign this learning to the piece you are studying, practicing it repeatedly until it is mastered.

For fast and difficult tempi, you have three choices:

- to start slowly and gradually increase tempo (but be aware that slower performances contain more errors, and slower speeds do not develop the muscle memory which has to be relearned once the correct tempo is achieved);

❑ to alternate slow and faster tempi;

❑ to practice at the correct tempo from the start.

Rescue Strategy

You should have a rescue strategy prepared, just in case. Like an insurance policy, you may never need it. To prepare your rescue strategy, do the following exercise:

Play a piece until you make a mistake. Keep going for a minute and then write down:

❑ *What do you do when you make a mistake (e.g. stop, carry-on, giggle, throw up your hands, squeal with horror, etc)?*

❑ *Where do you go tense in your body?*

❑ *What emotions do you feel?*

❑ *What thoughts do you have?*

- *Where does your focus go? (e.g. Is there anyone you imagine chastising you? Do you think about the impact on press reviews? Etc.)*

- *Finally, what thoughts, feelings, physical sensations would be of greatest assistance in developing your resilience? Write them down under three separate headings ~ Thoughts, Feelings and Physical. Anchor them using a word or phrase, choosing one which is a neutral anchor e.g. 'It's OK', 'Keep going', 'Let it go', 'Bin!' or 'Recover'.*

2. During Performance

In a performance you have no choice but to accept the mistake and move swiftly on. Whatever your feelings may be, they are totally irrelevant at this moment and cannot be indulged; they can be dealt with later. Your Rescue Strategy will have prepared you for dealing with this eventuality, so immediately get back into the present by:

❑ Focussing on what you are doing, hearing, and seeing NOW. Thinking back to what has just happened, or forward to what might happen is potentially calamitous. So, bring your attention onto what your body is doing right now ~ if you are an instrumentalist, focus on your fingers and your instrument, if you are a singer, concentrate on your throat and mouth; listen to the sound you are producing second by second; visually bring your attention right on to the conductor or your instrument.

- ❏ Relax your key muscles by breathing and relaxing.

- ❏ Use the auditory anchor with which your anchored the thoughts, feelings and sensations you prepared at the end of your Rescue Strategy.

- ❏ Play within your comfort zone as "compensating" for an error with a spectacular display of virtuosity is more likely to compound the problem.

3. After Performance

<u>Now</u> is the time that you can let go and allow the feelings you have been having to emerge. When that 'now' is, will depend upon prevailing conditions. If you are a soloist who is to attend a civic reception after the concert, your feelings may have to stay on hold for its duration. When that moment comes, you should allow the feelings to

bubble up – anger, rage, sadness, self-pity, powerlessness – allow them out. When they have subsided and you are feeling calmer, you can:

- ❑ Put the mistake into perspective (see earlier).

- ❑ Ask yourself which word in your "mistake vocabulary" is appropriate.

- ❑ Check that you have not set too high expectations of yourself.

- ❑ Remind yourself that making a mistake is about behaviour, not about your identity. It is a mistake, it is NOT the person you are. Repeat to yourself ten times: "What I do is not who I am".

Once your immediate feelings have been dealt with, the performance should be reviewed and reframed.

Reviewing Mistakes

Clanger or booboo, there is something for you to learn from what happened. There is a saying in NLP :

> **"There is no such thing as failure, only feedback".**

Understanding this can be transformational. Regarding your mistake as feedback is completely different from regarding it as failure. I describe failure as a fat word; that is, a word which is overused and abused and one which seems to hold far too much weight; it is an inflated word redolent with meaning and overtones of school exams, driving tests and getting the sack. Feedback, by contrast is a thin word – fit, lean, agile and flexible.

Rejoice!! You have feedback! Feedback that something isn't working (in this instance) and your task now is to explore what precisely and objectively you can learn. See it as a continuous loop in which the feedback from one performance feeds forward into the next:

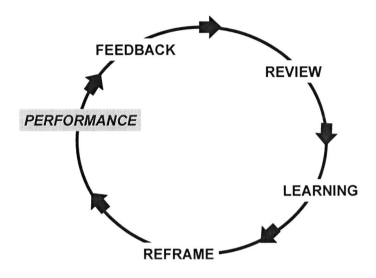

Avoid:

- Asking the question Why? It is not a helpful question because it produces circular thinking. Why? Because it is a hand-wringing, head-shaking sort of question. Why? Because it usually results in a prolonged bout of self-flagellation. Why? Because that's usually followed by mental pain. Why? Because the question is sometimes unanswerable. Why? Shut up! Move on!

- Comparing yourself with others and making generalisations:

  - "I'm not as good as..........."

  - "I'm always making mistakes" (always?)

  - " .... never makes mistakes" (never?)

Instead, take yourself through a series of 'useful' questions:

- **Environment:** What was the physical setting? Where were you exactly? What were you wearing? What could you have changed? How might you have managed those things you could not change more effectively?

- **Behaviour:** What specifically were you doing at the time the mistake occurred? What were you not doing that you could have been doing? What could you have done differently?

- **Capability:** Did you have the skills necessary to play this piece or this passage? Have you over-stretched yourself? Had you prepared adequately – technically, physically, mentally, emotionally? What might you have done (or not done) that would have increased your capability?

- **Beliefs:** What are your beliefs about the mistake? What were your beliefs before the performance? Are there any limiting beliefs you need to change?

- **Identity:** How intact is your sense of self? Has this experience damaged your self-esteem?

Reframing Mistakes

Having acquired an understanding of the situation, move on to reframe your experience. This is a modified and simplified version of the Fast Phobia Cure.

Relax and prepare to watch an imaginary video of your performance.

From a dissociated perspective (watching yourself from a distance on a screen) view the mistake(s) again from just <u>before</u> the mistake to just <u>afterwards</u> when you had recovered.

Run the scene backwards.

Break state (breathe, stand up etc).

Run the scene backwards again, but faster. Repeat 3 times getting faster.

How do you feel about it now?

If you feel no better, associate into the film just after you made the mistake, run it backwards fast (working up to the speed of a hand clap), 3 times.

This will scramble or decode your memory.

Whatever you needed to do, see yourself achieving it expertly and effortlessly <u>without mistakes</u> on a new film, dissociated.

When you are completely satisfied with this new version, associate into it, and experience yourself performing perfectly.

Be totally associated – seeing, hearing, feeling what you see, hear and feel.

4. POST-PERFORMANCE AND AFTER

Post-Performance Review

The performance is over. You have been to the civic reception, got yourself home, dealt with your feelings about any blunders you made, and have gone over the performance in your mind many times.

There is a three step process you can go through:

1. Managing the post – performance feelings. the highs and lows.

2. Winding down after the performance, so that you can relax, sleep and move on.

3. Reviewing your successes and failures. Rushing on to the next performance and the one after without pausing to reflect means that

you are avoiding learning consciously from your own experience.

Post-Performance Feelings

You will have feelings after the performance, and whatever they are, they need to be dealt with so that they lose their power and their hold over you and are starved of attention.

An older Cherokee man is teaching his grandson about life. "A fight is going on inside me," he says to the boy. "It is a terrible fight and it is between two wolves. One is evil. He is anger, envy, sorrow, regret, greed, selfishness, arrogance, self pity, guilt, resentment, inferiority, lies, false pride, superiority and ego. The other is good. He is love, joy, peace, hope, serenity, humility, kindness, benevolence, empathy, generosity, truth, compassion and faith. This same fight is going on inside you and inside every other person."

> The grandson thinks about it for a minute and then asks his grandfather, "Which wolf will win?"
>
> The old Cherokee man replies, "The one you feed." [30]

If you are happy – express your joy, talk about it to others, hug those you feel closest to (even if some of them are surprised), shout, sing……….. and then begin to consciously calm yourself down through breathing more slowly and deeply using the 4-2-6-2 sequence.

If you are sad – you may need to cry. Do so. Crying lets go of sadness. It is nothing to be ashamed of – footballers do it, businessmen do it, I do it. You are not losing control – you are expressing and releasing a deeply felt feeling. Once you have cried, start breathing, 4-2-6-2.

If you are angry – shout and scream, bang cushions, pillows. If you are angry with a person, imagine that they

---

[30] Author unknown

are one of your cushions and beat the living daylights out of it / them. After the fight, breathe 4-2-6-2.

If you are muted and feel as if you don't have any feelings – I don't believe you! Ask yourself "What am I feeling right now?" If your answer is nothing, run down this list and circle any of them that resonate:

abandoned, abused, accepted, accused, admired, adventurous, affectionate, affirmed, afraid, aggressive, aggravated, agitated, alarmed, alienated, alive, alone, ambivalent, angry, annoyed, antagonistic, anticipated, anxious, apathetic, appreciated, apprehensive, approved, arrogant, ashamed, assertive, attacked, attractive, awed, awkward, balanced, beaten, belligerent, betrayed, bewildered, bitter, blamed, bored, bothered, bugged, burned up, capable, cared for, castrated, caustic, chagrined, challenged, cheated, closed, comfortable, comforted, compassionate, competent, complacent, compromised, concerned, confident, confused, congruent, connected, consumed, contaminated, controlled, out of control, creative, cross, cruel, crushed, curious, cut off, dead, deceived, defeated, defensive, defiant, degraded, dejected, delighted, deserving, desired, desperate, destroyed, devastated, dirty, disappointed, discontented, disgusted, disillusioned, disjointed, dismayed, distant, distorted, distracted, distressed, disturbed, dominated, domineering, drained, dread, drowning, drugged, dumb, dying, eager, edgy, egotistic, elated, embarrassed, embraced, empty, endangered, enraged, enthused, envious, evasive, exasperated, exhausted, exhilarated, exploited, explosive, exposed, failed, failure, fat, fatigued, fearful, fighting mad, floundering, fooled, forgiven, forgotten, fouled, free, friendless, friendly, frightened, frustrated, furious, galled, generous, genuine, gifted, gracious, grateful, gratified, greedy, grumpy, guilty, hate, hated, hatred, healed, heavy, helpless, hopeful, hopeless, hostile, hurt, hyperactive, hypercritical, hypocritical, ignored, immobilized, impatient, impotent, inadequate, indifferent, incompetent, inconsistent, in control, indecisive, independent, indignant, inferior, infuriated, inhibited, injured, insecure, irked, irritated, isolated, intense, integrated, intimate, intimidated, irrational, irritable, jealous, joyful, judged, judgmental, liberated, light, limited, lonely, like a loser, lost, lovable, loved, loyal, mad, manipulated, marked, masked, masochistic, melancholic, miffed, misinformed, misunderstood, naked, needy, neglected, noxious, obligated, offended, optimistic, outraged, overlooked, oversized, overwhelmed, pain, panic, paranoid, passionate, peaceful, persecuted, perturbed, pessimistic, phoney, pissed-off, playful, pleased, pleasured, possessed, possessive, powerful, powerless, precious, preoccupied, pressured, private, protective, proud, provoked, punished, purposeful, put down, put out, puzzled, rage, rambunctious, reassured, rejected, resentful, responsible, responsive, restrained, resurrected, revengeful, reverence, rewarded, rigid, sacred, sad, sadistic, scape-goated, scared, secretive, secure, seductive, seething, selfish, shaky, shamed, shocked, shy, sick, sincere, sinful, smothered, soiled, sorrowful, spontaneous, spiteful, stressed, strong, stubborn, stupid, subservient, superior, supported, suspicious, sympathetic, tender, terrified, threatened, ticked off, tired, tolerant, tolerated, traumatized, tranquil, triumphant, trusted, trusting, turned off, ugly, unable, unappreciated, unbalanced, uncertain, understood, unfulfilled, unhappy, unique, unloved, unprepared, upset, unresponsive, unlikeable, uptight, used, useful, useless, vain, valuable, vengeful, vicious, vindicated, vindictive, violent, vulnerable, warm, weak, weary, whole, withdrawn, wonderful, worn out, worthless, worthy, youthful, yearning, zany, zealous [31]

So, you do have feelings after all!! If it truly is the case that you have none, move on to the next stage; if however you have found a teeny-weeny feeling, express it in whatever way is appropriate and then breathe yourself down to earth, 4-2-6-2.

---

[31] List taken from "*A partial list of feelings*", see www.ascasupport.org/3005a-i-mt-feel.htm

Winding Down

A performing day can be a long one, involving travel, rehearsal, performance, more travel. However tired you feel at the end of it, you may find it difficult to unwind when you get to bed with your mind scanning back through the performance. Do one of the relaxation exercises described earlier.

Reviewing Successes And Setbacks

Don't forget – this is feedback, and whether it was a good performance or a poor one there will be things you can learn; however good it was there will be something you could have done differently. In the same way that a bad performance is not just a chance happening, neither is a good one.

The review will be a pleasant or unpleasant experience depending on your judgment and perception of the performance, and it is important to do the review dissociated. When you have done the review, you can decide what you would like to do differently, see yourself doing it dissociated before associating into it and imprinting it in your unconscious.

If you have made what you regard as being a really serious mistake, you should do the Reframing Exercise in Chapter 10.

Imagine that your performance has been recorded on video. But you are able to view yourself performing in any colour, at any distance, and from any perspective.

Watch the performance rolling on the screen and notice, notice, notice without any criticism or judgement. Notice what you are doing and how you are doing it.

After the review, think about:

❑ *What you did?*

□ *What you can learn?*

□ *What you might (or might not) have done differently?*

□ *What, if anything, was missing or superfluous?*

Imprinting a perfect performance

Now create a new video of yourself giving the perfect performance. This will add to your stock of "greatest hits" videos which can be viewed at any time (and free of charge)! Change anything and everything that will enable you to perform perfectly. Do this dissociated, watching yourself on the screen until you have perfected all aspects. All is excellent. You are in total control of this movie, you are writer, star performer, producer and director, so be satisfied only with the very, very best.

When it is as perfect as perfect can be, associate into it, seeing what you see, hearing what you hear, feeling what you feel. Allow your body, your mind and your emotions to be as engaged in this performance as is possible.

You now have a recording of this supremely excellent performance stored in your memory. But more than that, you have a resource you can call upon at any time; you can use it before your next engagement and all future performances, or before you play some or all of the same repertoire again.

Chapter 12
Over To You

It's Up To You Now

I've done my bit; I've given you all the tools you need to be mentally robust and to perform at your peak at all times. You have read, or dipped into, this book. Now it is up to you. You have a choice – to use this book, to use it as a guide and to have it as your constant companion (as vital to your career as your instrument, your voice or hands) or, to carry on as you have always done, getting the results you've always got. It is a choice and it is your choice.

Building And Maintaining Mental Resilience

As a musician it may have taken you a long time to realise that practice produces results. There is no athlete who can compete without adequate training; no marathon runner who can build the staying power and resilience without many hours pounding the pavements or roads; and no musician who can walk on to a platform without having first rehearsed what they are going to do. In the same way, mental stamina requires training and practice until it becomes unconsciously competent, such that you do it without thinking about it (as you would brake when a traffic light turns red).

Practice, practice, practice. And when you've done that, practice again. Practice relaxation, visualisation, affirmations, anchoring, reinforce the Circle Of Excellence. Practice in harmless, non-threatening circumstances and gradually raise the stakes, until you are able to use these skills in the most stressful of circumstances.

Re-run regularly the video of your perfect performance. This is a powerful resource, use it.

And, oh yes, don't forget, enjoy your music making! However elevated the level at which you perform, do not lose sight of the fact that music is entertainment, it is an art to be enjoyed by the creator and the consumer.

I wish you joy.

Performance Issues And Recommended Solutions
A List Of Exercises And Techniques

Performance Issue	Recommended Solution	
Current performing state	Performance matrix	Ch 3
	Baseline performing state	Ch 7
Reducing anxiety and tension	Breathing	Ch 4
	Progressive muscular relaxation	Ch 5
	Shortened progressive muscular relaxation	Ch 5
	Simple relaxation routine	Ch 5
	Cued relaxation	Ch 5
	NLP self hypnosis	Ch 5
	4 stage self hypnosis	Ch 5
	Guided relaxation	Ch 5
Learning new repertoire	Mental rehearsal	Ch 6
Reducing unpleasant memories	Dissociation	Ch 6

Increasing pleasant memories	Association	Ch 6
Changing state	Anchoring states	Ch 7
Changing negative thoughts to positive	Visual switch	Ch 7
Limiting beliefs	Changing limiting beliefs	Ch 7
		Ch 7
	Affirmations	
Critical inner voice	Silencing the inner critic	Ch7
		Ch 7
	Recognising the Critic subpersonality	Ch 7
	Affirmations	Ch 7
Fearful experiences	Fast Phobia Cure	Ch 7
Creating a practice routine	Practice routines	Ch 8
Planning practice	Practice plan	Ch 8
	Practice warm up routine	Ch 9
	Mental rehearsal of practice	Ch 9
Managing practice time	Practice plan	Ch 8
Pre-performance	Pre-performance	Ch 8

routine	routines	
Anchoring	Circle of Excellence	Ch 9
performance states	Piece of Cake	Ch 9
and qualities		
Day of performance	Checklist	Ch 9
	Preparation	Ch 9
	Venue checklist	Ch 9
Dealing with	Black box technique	Ch 10
distractions		
Developing	Switching focus	Ch 10
concentration		
Mistakes	Developing a Rescue	Ch 12
	Strategy	Ch 12
	Reframing	
Dealing with post-		Ch 12
performance feelings		
Winding down after	Progressive muscular	Ch 5
performance	relaxation	
	Guided relaxation	Ch 5
Perfect performance		Ch 12
imprint		
Reviewing		Ch 12
performance		

Bibliography and resources

Andreas, S., and Faulkner, C., *NLP The New Technology of Achievement,* Nicholas Brealey Publishing, 1994

Assagioli, Roberto, *The Act of Will,* Harper & Row, 1990

Baum. K., *The Mental Edge,* Perigee, 1999

Cannon, Walter B., (1914) The emergency function of the adrenal medulla in pain and the major emotions. *American Journal of Physiology* 33: 356-372

Cannon, Walter B., (1932). *The wisdom of the body*, 2nd Edition, 1939, Norton Pubs, New York

Emmons, S., and Thomas, A., *Power performance for singers,* Oxford University Press, 1998

Ferrucci, P., *What We May Be,* Turnstone Press, 1982

Green, B., and Gallwey, W. T., *The Inner Game of Music*, Doubleday, 1986

Greene, Don., *Performance Success*, Routledge, 2002

Jones, G., Hanton, S., & Connaughton, D. (2002). What is this thing called mental toughness? An investigation of elite sport performers. *Journal of Applied Sport Psychology, 14,* 205-218.

Kennerley, H., *Managing Anxiety, A User's Manual,* Oxford University Press

Loehr, James, E., *Mental toughness training for sports,* R.R. Donnelley & Sons, 1987

McDermott, I., *The NLP Practitioner Programme,* ITS, 2002-3

McDermott, I., *The NLP Master Practitioner Programme,* ITS, 2003

Merriam-Webster's Medical Dictionary, Merriam-Webster, Inc., 2002

How To Cope With Panic Attacks, Mind Publications, 2000

How To Increase Your Self-Esteem, Mind Publications, 2001

How To Stop Worrying, Mind Publications, 2001

Nideffer, R., *Psyched to Win.* Leisure Press, 1992.

O'Connor, Joseph., *NLP & Sports,* Thorsons, 2001

O'Connor, Joseph., *NLP Workbook,* Thorsons, 2001

Reber, Arthur, S., *The Penguin Dictionary of Psychology,* Penguin Books, 1985

Seth, Vikram, *An Equal Music,* Phoenix House, 1999

Simonton, O. C., Simonton, S. M., and Creighton, J. I., *Getting Well Again,* Bantam, 1992

Syer, J., and Connolly, C., *Sporting Body, Sporting Mind: An Athlete's Guide to Mental Training,* Simon & Schuster Ltd, 1987

Understanding Anxiety, Mind Publications, 2001

Westbrook, D., and Rouf, K., *Understanding Panic,* Oxford Cognitive Therapy Centre, 1995

Williamon, A., *Musical Excellence*, Oxford University Press, 2004

Index

Affirmations	**124-126**
Alexander Technique	**57-58**
Anchors	73, 74, 103, **108-116**, 117, 121-124, 162, 166-169, 200, 202, 222, 225, 226
Andreas, Steve	170, 227
Anxiety	20, 22, 32-36, 45,46, 52, 57, 98, 134, 224, 227, 228
Arousal	32, 42, 42, 53, 54, 162
Assagioli, Roberto	28, 128, 227
Association	**103-107,** 225
Attention model	**187-189**
Attunement	**161-163**
Autogenic Therapy	**55-56**
Bandler, Richard	133, 170

Behaviour	17, 18, 19, 20, 95, 127, 133, 203, 207
Black Box technique	**181-184**
Breathing	8, 16, 21, 22, 34, **39-50,** 52, 56, 64 85, 86, 88, 90, 102, 111, 162, 170, 202, 213,224
Cannon, Walter	40, 227
Carlyle, Thomas	152
Chaining anchors	**115-116**
Changing state	**95-141**, 225
Cherokee folktale	212-213
Circle of Excellence	**166-169,** 172, 178, 222, 226
Concentration	12, **29,** 34, 36, **181-191,** 226
Connolly, Christopher	181, 228
Conscious mind	**16-20**
Cued relaxation	**63-64**
Decision destroyer	170
Dissociation	**103-107,** 133, 224

DIY relaxation	**58-68**
Drink	177, 178, 179
Emmons, Shirlee, and Thomas, Alma	32, 227
Emotional balance	**26-27**
Fast Phobia Cure	133, 135, 141, 208, 225
Faulkner, Charles	170, 227
Feedback	7, **204-205,** 217
Feelings	
-affect performance	**13-16**
-and unconscious mind	16
-list of	**214-216**
Feldenkrais Method	**56**
Ferrucci, Piero	128, 130, 227
Fight or flight syndrome	21, **40-41,** 55
Findhorn	161
Ford, Henry	15-16
Franck, Cesar	14
Freud, Sigmund	17

Gallwey, Tim	7, 29-31, 227
Goran-Eriksson, Sven	6
Green, Barry, and Gallwey, Tim	7, 30, 227
Greene, Don	39, 227
Grinder, John	133
Guided Relaxation	**68-74**
Hallbom, Tim	169
Happich, Hans	81
Hypnosis	18, 21, 135
-self-hypnosis	**64-68**
Hypnotic trance	21
Inner Game, The	**29-30,** 227
Interference	**29-31,** 39
Jacobson, Edmund	58, 59, 79
Jones, G., Hanton, S., & Connaughton, D.	7, 227
Lapses	
- language of	**194-196**
- perception of	**192-194**

Limiting beliefs	**118-126,** 207, 225
Loehr, James	10, 227
McDermott, Ian	99, 120, 228
Meals	179
Mental health	**4-7**
Mental rehearsal	22, **76-94,** 159, 162, 176, 178, 224, 225
Mental skills	8, 9, **10-23,** 26, 32, 33, 37
Mental resilience	8, 9, **39-141**
Merriam-Webster Medical Dictionary	29, 228
Mistakes	
- language of	**194-196**
- managing	**191-203**
- perception of	**192-194**
- reframing	**208-209**
- reviewing	**203-207**
Negative thoughts	**116-118**
Neuro Linguistic Programming (NLP)	3, 19, 24, 25, 58, 65, 95, 99, 120,

	133-135, 169, 170, 203, 224, 227, 228
Nicklaus, Jack	80
Nideffer, Robert	39, 187, 228
-stress model	**39-40**
-attention model	**187-189**
O'Connor, Joseph	3, 19, 25, 26, 65, 120, 228
Performance	13-18, 20, **181-209**
Performing cycle	13
Performing state	**24-37, 98-102**
Piece of Cake	**169-170,** 172, 226
Pillars of performing success	3-4
Positive thoughts	19, 29, **116-118,** 170
Post-performance	**211-220**
Practice	8, 9, 12, 23, 75, 79, 83, **143-156**
Practice schedule	**145-151,** 152, 153, 160
Pre-performance	**157-180**
Progressive Muscular Relaxation	**59-63,** 224, 226

Psychosynthesis	28, 128
Reframing	**208-209,** 218, 226
Relaxation	8, 12, 22, 26, 27, 34, 35, 36, 42, 43, 50, **51-74,** 79, 86, 88, 90, 135, 159, 162, 176, 217, 222, 224, 226
Reviewing	104, **203-207,** 211, **217-220**, 226
Rewind Technique	135
Roll, Michael	192-194
Royal College of Music	143, 153
Simonton, Carl, and Stephanie	81, 228
Seth, Vikram	163, 228
Smith, Suzi	169
Sport psychology	6, 10, 78, 227
Stacking anchors	**115-116**
State	
-baseline	**98-102**
-changing	**102-116**
-current performing	**33-37**

-ideal performing	**27-37**
Stress	5, 12, 21, **39-43,** 44, 46, 53, 57
Stress model	**39-40**
Subpersonalities	**127-132**
Syer, John	181, 228
Thomas, Alma (and Emmons, Shirlee)	32, 227
Thoughts	13, 14, 16, 18, 19, 20, 23, 32, 95, **116-118,** 170, 190, 199, 200, 202, 225
Time management	145, **153-156**
Unconscious mind	**16-21,** 68, 81, 86, **106,** 113, 121, 122, 124, 125, 170
V-K Dissociation Process	133
Visualisation	8, 22, 54, **75-94,** 103, 222
Visual Switch	**117-118,** 225
Warm up routine	145, 159, 160, **161-164,** 178, 225
Will	**27-29**

Williamon, Aaron   143, 228

Yerkes-Dodson Law   **42-43**

Zoning-In project   143

Printed in the United Kingdom
by Lightning Source UK Ltd.
123004UK00001B/97/A

9 781904 312222